PRAISE FOR *AN APPLIED* 1
GUIDE TO RESEARCH DESIGNS

"The array of approaches is impressively inclusive; an excellent guide for a student seeking a methodology."

—Ralph E. Swan, *Chestnut Hill College*

"The strength of this text lies in its succinct go-to style. For me, it is like the APA Publication Manual in that it will be a resource not only for classroom learning, but also for faculty research and article review."

—John L. Garland, *Alabama State University*

"The presentation of research scenario examples, including design and probable statistical analyses, is one thing often missing in general research texts. I also like the design and analyses depicted in pictorial/graphical format, which allows ease in understanding."

——Rebecca Keele, *New Mexico State University*

"The topics progress in a logical order, although [the book] allows flexibility to read stand-alone topics. It is a reference text that one can readily turn to and refer to as a guide."

—Theodore D. Joseph, *Paine College*

"The text does have two distinct strengths: It covers in depth a topic that needs to be addressed, and few other books have this level of detail; and it does a very nice job of visually presenting various examples of research design. This text is both practical and useful for students."

—Peter M. Jonas, *Cardinal Stritch University*

"This text's information is readily accessible and organized with great examples to guide students. The literature-based examples are really helpful."

—Betty Carter Dorr, *Fort Lewis College*

"It fills a huge void in the field of psychology in providing students and professors with a survey of research designs that are most appropriate to answering the many different and wide-ranging questions that students are now interested in pursuing."

—Cynthia E. Winston, *Howard University*

An Applied Reference Guide to Research Designs

I'd like to dedicate this book to all my past supervisors, professors, teachers, and dedicated students. They have provided me the support, skills, interest, and motivation to continue the lines of scholarly work and achievement in a never ending effort to expand our minds.

—Alex Edmonds

I would like to dedicate this book to my wife Karen and my three boys, Aiden, Ethan, and Ashton.

—Tom Kennedy

An Applied Reference Guide to
Research Designs

Quantitative, Qualitative, and Mixed Methods

W. Alex Edmonds
Tom D. Kennedy

Nova Southeastern University

Los Angeles | London | New Delhi
Singapore | Washington DC

Los Angeles | London | New Delhi
Singapore | Washington DC

FOR INFORMATION:

SAGE Publications, Inc.
2455 Teller Road
Thousand Oaks, California 91320
E-mail: order@sagepub.com

SAGE Publications Ltd.
1 Oliver's Yard
55 City Road
London EC1Y 1SP
United Kingdom

SAGE Publications India Pvt. Ltd.
B 1/I 1 Mohan Cooperative Industrial Area
Mathura Road, New Delhi 110 044
India

SAGE Publications Asia-Pacific Pte. Ltd.
33 Pekin Street #02-01
Far East Square
Singapore 048763

Acquisitions Editor: Vicki Knight
Editorial Assistant: Kalie Koscielak
Production Editor: Catherine M. Chilton
Copy Editor: Tina Hardy
Typesetter: C&M Digitals (P) Ltd.
Proofreader: Tracy Villano
Indexer: Marilyn Augst
Cover Designer: Krishnan Anupama
Marketing Manager: Helen Salmon
Permissions Editor: Adele Hutchinson

Copyright © 2013 by SAGE Publications, Inc.

Printed in the United States of America

Library of Congress Cataloging-in-Publication Data

Edmonds, W. Alex.

An applied reference guide to research designs : quantitative, qualitative, and mixed methods / W. Alex Edmonds, Thomas D. Kennedy.

p. cm.
Includes bibliographical references and index.

ISBN 978-1-4522-0509-0 (pbk.)

1. Social sciences—Research—Methodology.
2. Education—Research—Methodology.
3. Research—Methodology. I. Kennedy, Thomas D. II. Title.

H62.E327 2013
001.4'2—dc23   2011031316

This book is printed on acid-free paper.

11 12 13 14 15 10 9 8 7 6 5 4 3 2 1

Brief Contents

Contents

List of Tables,
Figures, and Diagrams

◆ TABLES

◆ FIGURES

DIAGRAMS ♦

Foreword

Research methods in the social sciences (I include behavioral sciences and education under this broader term) are quite varied, as the number of settings and situations in which our investigations occur are immense. Furthermore, concerns about research ethics and potential harm inflicted on human subjects put severe limits on what is feasible, requiring social scientists to have at their disposal a plethora of possible approaches to apply to a given problem. Social scientists, particularly those who do nonexperimental research and those who conduct field research in naturalistic settings, must be well versed in many varied methods in order to be prepared to apply optimal approaches to address their research questions in specific settings. Although different disciplines within social science have developed some of their own approaches and practices, there is a great deal of overlap among disciplines in the methodologies utilized.

One can classify methods according to whether they are qualitative or quantitative. Although there are a variety of approaches, qualitative methods are distinguished by their collection and synthesis of information in a largely nonquantitative way. For example, individuals might be interviewed about their experiences living in a college dormitory. The researcher will review and synthesize the responses, looking for meaningful themes. Quantitative methods, on the other hand, tend to involve defining variables in advance and then quantifying observations of those variables. Thus, one might ask college students to complete a survey in which questions ask for ratings about various aspects of the dormitory experience, such as how much they liked the food on a 1 to 5 scale. Different disciplines within social science tend to favor one approach over the other, for example, anthropologists make frequent use of qualitative methods whereas psychologists mainly use quantitative methods, although there are exceptions on both sides.

The quantitative methods training in social science often divides methodology into assessment, design, and statistics. Assessment concerns techniques for measuring or operationalizing variables largely using multiple-item psychological tests and scales. Design is the structure of an investigation that defines the sequence and nature of both the conditions subjects are exposed to and the observations taken on those subjects. Statistics concerns the mathematical procedures used to analyze the quantitative data produced by the study once the design is implemented. Assessment, design, and statistics are all important elements in any quantitative investigation, so students must develop expertise in all three. Certainly one must have sound measurement to be able to draw conclusions about the underlying variables of interest, and one must analyze data using appropriate statistics, but it is the *design* of the investigation that is most important in being able to draw inferences from an investigation.

This book deals primarily with design, including both designs for experimental and nonexperimental research. It is perhaps unique in providing a balanced treatment of both qualitative and quantitative methods that are integrated at the end when mixed methods are discussed. The book begins with a general discussion of basic principles of the scientific method in social science, including topics such as validity and control. It then covers quantitative methods, including experimental, quasi-experimental (in Part I), and nonexperimental (in Part II) research. Part III discusses a variety of qualitative methods, including grounded theory, ethnography, narrative, and phenomenological approaches. The book concludes (Part IV) with a treatment of mixed methods that involves elements of both qualitative and quantitative methods.

This book includes both basic and advanced designs, making it useful as both a textbook for students in a course that covers design and as a guide to experienced researchers. The book provides an example from the literature for every design covered. A brief overview is provided of each example study's research question and procedure, as well as recommended statistical approaches for data analysis. The citation is provided from widely available journals so each article can be consulted for more details. Thus, the reader can easily see how each research team was able to use each design and how those researchers handled data analysis and interpretation.

Although not every social scientist will use all of these designs, the serious student of social science research methodology needs a basic understanding of how design features inform appropriate inference. Such a student should have a working knowledge of qualitative and quantitative methods, as provided in this book. It can provide an introduction to design that can later serve as a reference to details of specific designs that can be applied to a particular problem. The development of the computer over the past three decades has shifted much of the focus of social scientists, especially those who do quantitative studies, from design to statistics as increasing computing power has allowed the development of increasingly computationally complex statistical methods.

Thus, in graduate programs we find many classes on statistics but few on design. It is important to remember that it is the *design* and *not* the statistic that is the basis for inference, making the study of design of vital importance, and this book is an invaluable resource for both social scientists and aspiring social scientists.

Paul E. Spector, PhD
University of South Florida

Preface

The objective of this reference book is to visually present, with consistent terminology, quantitative, qualitative, and mixed methods research designs in education and the social and behavioral sciences in a way that students and researchers can readily understand and accurately apply in their own investigations. Through our experience and research for this guide, we realized there are many inconsistencies and variations of terminology, both within and between research texts in education and the social and behavioral sciences, especially with the use of the terms *method, research, approach,* and *design.* We believe that the terminology should be clearly distinguished with the appropriate nomenclature. The interchange of terminology creates confusion among consumers of research, particularly students. We attempt to resolve the confusion by breaking down each aspect of the research terminology into its components in a hierarchical fashion to provide clarity for the reader. As seen in the chart that follows, the resulting nomenclature is thus used throughout the text.

Level	Explanation
METHOD₁	The *method* is the theoretical, philosophical, and data analytic perspective. The method can be quantitative, qualitative, or mixed (e.g., a quantitative method₁).
▼ RESEARCH₂	▼ *Research* refers to the systematic process of control (e.g., group assignment, selection, and data collection techniques). Research can be experimental, quasi-experimental, or nonexperimental (e.g., a quantitative method₁ and experimental research₂).
▼ APPROACH₃	▼ The *approach* is the first step to creating structure to the design, and it details (a) a theoretical model of how the data will be collected, and (b) if one case, one group, or multiple groups will be associated with the process (e.g., a quantitative method₁, experimental research₂ with a between-subjects approach₃).
▼ DESIGN₄	▼ The *design* is the actual structure or framework that indicates (a) the time frame(s) in which data will be collected or how and when the data will be analyzed using qualitative methods, (b) when the treatment will be implemented (or not), and (c) the exact number of groups that will be involved (e.g., a quantitative method₁, experimental research₂ with a between-subjects approach₃ and a pretest and posttest control group design₄).

This book is designed to improve one's ability to conceptualize, construct, test, problem solve, and acquire knowledge, all of which are characteristics of scientific inquiry and the creative process required when conducting research. We have discovered, in teaching research methods courses and supervising dissertation committees, that students often have a difficult time conceptualizing the most appropriate research design, en route to collecting the data and answering the stated research questions or hypotheses. Based on this observation, we sought to find the best text that could help resolve this critical issue. We found that most research methods texts are more broad, covering the entire spectrum of the research process while devoting only a single chapter, or a few sections embedded throughout (often incomplete), to research designs. Furthermore, the authors of these texts often present the research designs without quality visual representations and sound real-life examples. The issue is further confounded when investigators omit from the Methods portion of published manuscripts an accurate description of the research design that was employed.

We also discuss the issue of inconsistent terminology; for example, it is not unusual to see authors utilize the following terms interchangeably: a correlational method, correlational research, a correlational approach, or a correlational design. Although this may not be entirely wrong, it is not entirely accurate (or specific) and can lead to confusion. It would be more accurate to say all together in sequence, a quantitative method, nonexperimental research, an observational approach, and a predictive design (and then, of course, the correlational statistic or regression analysis is applied to the observational data). These inconsistencies, at best, can lead to confusion and difficulties when attempting to conceptualize and choose the design that best fits the research problem and subsequent questions or hypotheses; at worst, they can render findings invalid. Considering these aspects, students often find themselves lost at that critical part of the research process while attempting to (a) choose a design that will allow for the acquisition of data best suited to answer their research questions or examine their hypotheses and (b) incorporate a design into the Procedures section of their Methods chapter of their dissertation.

Although we cover a variety of practical research designs in quantitative, qualitative, and mixed methods, this book is not intended to be a complete reference guide for individuals conducting program evaluations. We briefly address this issue at the end of this guide. We revealed through our research for this book that many of these sound research designs presented within are underutilized in education and the social and behavioral sciences. We hope the presentation of these materials will continue to strengthen research in the area through the application of sound methodological techniques. These designs can be applied in field, laboratory, and even web-based settings. Although this book does not go into great detail regarding the theory or philosophy of qualitative or quantitative methods and the associated research designs, we do provide recommended texts and articles for the reader who is interested in a more thorough understanding of a particular approach, method, or design. The intent of this book is seemingly paradoxical, in that we attempt to give students and researchers a dense (no filler), yet quick reference guide for conceptualizing and creating a design that best fits the primary research question. Thus, this is an applied text, using visual aids and real-world examples, rather than covering foundational and theoretical issues.

Visually delivering the information coupled with relevant examples may optimize the learning process and subsequent application of learning. The reader will notice that we often state that further decisions about the applications of particular research designs should be based on "theoretical and logistical considerations." Although we attempt to apply linear logic and black and white elements to scientific methodology, there are many instances in which "rules of thumb" and old laws do not apply. Research in the field of social sciences is still relatively new, and the vast and varied contexts in which we investigate create a level of complexity and sophistication that often requires subjectivity and interpretation.

As mentioned earlier, this book is meant to cover the most practical and common research designs currently used in educational and the social and behavioral sciences. Referring to these research designs as "common" or "practical" is somewhat a misnomer, and it does not imply that the designs are less powerful or the results have less meaning. In reviewing many articles over the years, we have noticed that, all too often, researchers use unnecessarily complex research designs that complicate the application and subsequent statistical analyses, leaving much more room for error. Parsimony is a favorable word in science; that is, a design should be as complex as it needs to be and, at the same time, as simple as it needs to be.

AUDIENCE ♦

The target audience for this book is the researcher in the fields of education, sociology, psychology, nursing, and other human-service fields. More specifically, this book is written for undergraduate students working on honors theses and for graduate students working on theses or dissertations. This book will assist all students who (a) have a basic understanding of research methods, (b) are in the process of conducting research, or (c) plan on conducting research at some point during their careers. Furthermore, it can also be used as a tool by professors who are either teaching research courses or supervising students on theses and dissertations. Specifically, professors will find this reference guide useful in assisting and guiding students interested in improving their understanding of how research is set up and conducted. We have attempted to create a visual system in the form of a practical, easy-to-follow reference guide to help in the conceptualization and development of many of the common research designs. We offer examples of this visual system "in action" for each of the designs presented with the use of published studies. In addition, further recommendations and suggestions are provided for those interested in acquiring a more comprehensive understanding of basic research designs. The book includes the core designs that are used by quantitative, qualitative, and mixed method researchers.

FEATURES ♦

We have maintained a singular focus on research designs and have provided an example for each chosen research design with a relevant peer-reviewed article. We have incorporated a number of features throughout the book that will assist students in designing their own studies. In each example, we summarize the procedures and include the relevant variables in a design notation model. In many cases, the research-article examples include multiple research questions or hypotheses. However, for the sake of clarity, we attempt to present one overarching research question that summarizes the major goal of the study. In some instances, for research in qualitative methods, we include a research aim. Research utilizing mixed methods usually contains an additional research question to answer the inquiry associated with combining quantitative results and qualitative findings. In addition to the example research designs, we also include brief discussions on (a) the relevant aspects of research, (b) different types of designs, (c) the scientific method, and (d) a list of recommended readings pertaining to each area. Also, located in the appendixes, we present many examples of rarely applied research designs, as well as case study designs, with brief notations on the intended use and effectiveness.

Unique Features

We have summarized and condensed over 130 articles and books included in this reference guide. In addition, there are many unique features associated with this guide. These features were included to enhance the understanding of the concepts and designs presented:

- An array of relevant references and sources for the reader
- Consistent terminology, which is emphasized throughout (a standardized taxonomy)
- Discussions on the differences between within- and between-subject approaches
- The use of the k-factor design as a means to distinguish multiple-treatment groups
- Inclusion of both within-subjects and between-subjects k-factor designs
- Diagrams of factorial designs
- Examples of the Solomon N-group designs as an extension of the four-group design
- Diagrams of single-case approaches
- Diagrams of nonexperimental research such as observational (correlational) and survey approaches
- Visual models for qualitative methods
- Proposed designs for mixed-method single-case approaches
- Appendixes covering examples of rarely used, but relevant, research designs for experimental and quasi-experimental research, case studies, and mixed methods

COMPANION WEBSITE ◆

For individuals interested in accessing links to the full-text articles related to each research design presented within, among many other relevant articles referenced in this guide, we direct those readers to the companion website, *A Cross-Section of Research Articles Classified by Design: Quantitative, Qualitative, and Mixed Methods.* This website contains links to the actual journal articles or the home pages of journals where the full-text articles can be accessed. Most articles can be accessed through a university's library database or through the library's associated interlibrary loan system. For referenced books, when available, we provide the home pages of the companion websites of the texts we have referenced in our book. For books that do not have companion websites, we provide the link to the home page of the publisher of the book, which provides more information about how to access or purchase the book (http://www.sagepub.com/edmonds).

ACKNOWLEDGMENTS ◆

We would like to thank Daniel L. Stufflebeam, PhD, and Ronald J. Chenail, PhD, for providing their insight, thoughts, and suggestions to our book. Drs. Stufflebeam and Chenail's expertise in their respective areas is undeniable and ultimately helped strengthen the overall product. We would also like to thank Paul E. Spector, PhD, for his insight and contribution to this book. His dedication to the field of scientific inquiry is unwavering and we are honored to have him as a part of this project. We would like to thank Robert K. Yin, PhD, for his thoughts and suggestions, as well as Robert Greene for his editorial and formatting contributions. A special thanks goes to Vicki Knight at Sage for her support and dedication to the project. A number of reviewers provided useful and valuable feedback, which ultimately shaped the book: Theodore D. Joseph, Paine College; Michael B. Johnson, University of Tennessee at Chattanooga; Sharon Anderson Dannels, The George Washington University; Peter M. Jonas, Cardinal Stritch University; Richard E. Adams, Kent State University; Ronald E. Goldsmith, Florida State University; David P. Byers, Bellevue University; John L. Garland, Alabama State University; Ralph E. Swan, Chestnut Hill College; Wanda Wigfall-Williams, American University; Rebecca Keele, New Mexico State University; Detmar Straub, Georgia State University; Marie L. Loggia-Kee, National University; Gretchen Perbix, Minnesota State University at Mankato; Betty Carter Dorr, Fort Lewis College; and Cynthia E. Winston, Howard University.

About the Authors

W. Alex Edmonds, PhD, BCB, is currently a program professor in the Applied Research Center at Nova Southeastern University in North Miami Beach, Florida. He graduated from Florida State University and received his doctoral degree in Educational Psychology with a minor in Statistics and Measurement. Over the years, Dr. Edmonds has applied his knowledge of research design, measurement, and assessment in both field and laboratory examinations. He has published extensively in a variety of areas such as psychophysiology and educational psychology. His primary interest revolves around applying unique methodological and statistical techniques as a means to exploring the relationship between emotions and performance in a variety of domains. He also has over 10 years of experience in applying biofeedback in the field, as well as for research. While in graduate school, he conducted his field work with the track and field team at Florida State and started using biofeedback for research and practice during this time. He has utilized biofeedback extensively with various types of athletes for performance enhancement, as well as stress-regulation techniques for individuals with type 2 diabetes and pain management for patients suffering from chronic pain. Dr. Edmonds is certified through the Biofeedback Certification International Alliance in general biofeedback.

Tom D. Kennedy, PhD, BCB, is currently a professor in the department of Applied Research at Nova Southeastern University. He received his PhD in Counseling Psychology from the University of Miami and his MA in Clinical Psychology from Southern Methodist University. He has been a faculty member at NSU for five years where he has developed and taught research and statistics courses. He is the Institutional Review Board representative for the School of Education. His clinical experience consists of providing neuropsychological assessments, behavioral medicine interventions, and group therapy in inpatient and outpatient settings, including the following: the University of Texas Southwestern Medical Center, University of Miami Mailman Center for Child Development, Jackson Memorial Hospital, University of Miami Institute for Individual and Family Therapy, and the

Dallas County Jail. His research interests include two convergent tracks, one focusing on at-risk children and adolescents and the other exploring biofeedback and other complementary and alternative medicine interventions. He has been the recipient of multiple grants and provides evaluation and grant writing services for various organizations in south Florida. He has published and presented in the areas of juvenile crime, psychophysiology, and research methodology. Dr. Kennedy is a licensed psychologist and is certified through the Biofeedback Certification International Alliance in general biofeedback and maintains a small private practice.

CHAPTER 1

THE SCIENTIFIC METHOD AND RELEVANT COMPONENTS

All researchers who attempt to formulate conclusions from a particular path of inquiry use aspects of the scientific method, which can vary from field to field and method to method. The sound application of the scientific method allows researchers to reveal valid empirical findings. Within the social sciences, the general steps include the following: (a) state the problem, (b) formulate the hypothesis, (c) design the experiment, (d) make observations, (e) interpret data, (f) draw conclusions, and (g) accept or reject the hypothesis. All research in quantitative methods, from experimental to nonexperimental, should employ the steps of the scientific method in an attempt to produce reliable and valid results. This scientific method provides the framework for the steps involved in education and the social and behavioral sciences research.

The scientific method can be likened to an association of techniques rather than an exact formula; therefore, we expand the steps as a means to be more specific and relevant for research in education and the social sciences. As seen in Figure 1.1, these steps include the following: (a) Identify a Research Problem, (b) Establish the Theoretical Framework, (c) Indicate the Purpose and Research Questions (or hypotheses), (d) Develop the Methodology, (e) Collect the Data, (f) Analyze and Interpret the Data, and (g) Report the Results. This book targets the critical component of the scientific method referred to in Figure 1.1 as "Develop the Methodology," which is the point in the process when the appropriate research design is selected. We do not focus on prior aspects of the scientific method or any steps that come after the "Develop the Methodology" step, including discussions on the nature of knowledge, epistemology, ontology, and worldviews. Specifically, this book focuses on the conceptualization, selection, and application of common research designs in the field of education and the social and behavioral sciences. Again, it is important to note that the scientific method varies from each field of inquiry (and type of method). The technique presented here may not exactly follow the logic required for research using qualitative methods; however, the conceptualization of research designs remains the same. We refer the reader to Jaccard and Jacoby (2010) for a review on the various scientific approaches associated with qualitative methods, such as emergent- and discovery-oriented frameworks.

Figure 1.1　The Scientific Method

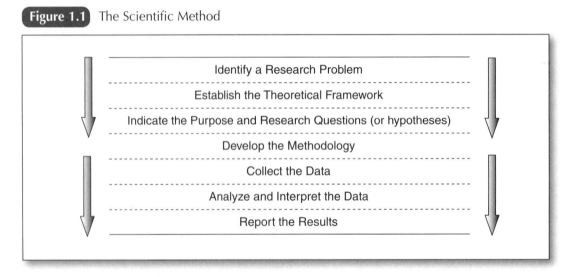

The primary purpose of a research design is to provide a conceptual framework that will allow the researcher to answer specific research questions, while utilizing sound principles of scientific inquiry. The concept behind research designs is intuitively straightforward, but applying these designs in real-life situations can be complex. More specifically, researchers face the challenge of (a) manipulating (or exploring) the social systems of interest, (b) utilizing measurement tools (or data collection techniques) that maintain adequate levels of validity and reliability, and (c) controlling the interrelationship between multiple variables or indicating emerging themes, which can lead to error in the form of confounding effects in the results.

Therefore, utilizing and following the tenets of a sound research design is one of the most fundamental aspects of the scientific method. Put simply, the research design is the structure of investigation, conceived so as to obtain the "answer" to research questions or hypotheses.

VALIDITY AND RESEARCH DESIGNS ♦

The overarching goal of research is to reach valid outcomes based upon the appropriate application of the scientific method. In reference to research designs, validity is defined as the extent to which the outcome accurately answers the stated research questions of the study. It is important to note that validity takes on many different forms, operates on a continuum, and theoretically can be considered multidimensional. Validity also has a place in psychometrics (i.e., the theories and techniques associated with educational and psychological measurements), and it is generally known as test validity. The validity of a measurement tool simply means that it measures what it is developed to measure. The focus within this reference guide is the validity related to research designs, *not* test validity (for more information related to test validity, reliability, and measurement, see DeVellis, [2003] and Viswanathan [2005]). Although securing validity is critical at the design stage, it should be a consideration throughout the general steps of the scientific method. The importance of securing "acceptable" levels of validity for research in quantitative methods cannot be overstated. However, aspects of validity have also been addressed for qualitative methods. Validity and the qualitative method include focusing in on the *trustworthiness* of the data and the rigor and quality of the data collection procedures (see Golafshani, 2003; Williams & Morrow, 2009). Additionally, the concept of external validity can have a place in qualitative methods as well. We refer the reader to Guba and Lincoln (2005) and Chenail (2010) for a review on nonprobabilistic approaches to aspects of generalizability for qualitative methods.

In the following paragraphs, we summarize four types of validity related to research designs for quantitative methods: internal, external, construct, and statistical conclusion validity. It should be noted that the concepts of internal, external, construct, and statistical conclusion validity were all originally conceptualized for the application and development of experimental and quasi-experimental research (Campbell, 1957; Cook & Campbell, 1979). Since that time, many researchers, books (e.g., Kazdin, 2002), and Internet references have attempted to classify and order these types of validity very differently in accordance with nonexperimental research, as well as within different disciplines (e.g., epidemiology). With minor additions, we organize and present the types of validity primarily based on Cook and Campbell's (1979) original work along with Shadish, Cook, and Campbell's (2002) composition. Any condition that compromises the validity related to a research design is known as a *threat* (i.e., confounding variables). All types of validity are applicable to experimental and quasi-experimental research; however, the conceptualization of internal validity (by definition) does *not* apply to nonexperimental research, including survey and observational (correlational) approaches. Another form of validity, statistical conclusion validity, applies to all research within quantitative methods and refers to the role of statistical analyses and its relation to research design.

Internal Validity

Internal validity is the extent to which the outcome was based on the independent variable (i.e., the treatment), as opposed to extraneous or unaccounted for variables. Specifically, internal validity has to do with causal inferences, hence the reason why it does not apply to nonexperimental research. The goal of nonexperimental research is to describe phenomena or to explain or predict the relationship between variables, not to infer causation (although there are circumstances when cause and effect can be inferred from nonexperimental research and this is discussed later in this guide). To identify any explanation that could be responsible for an outcome (effect) outside of the independent variable (cause) is considered to be a threat. The most common threats to internal validity seen in education and the social and behavioral sciences are detailed in Table 1.1. It should be noted that many texts do not indentify *sequencing effects* in the common lists of threats; however, this is placed here, as it is a primary threat in repeated-measures approaches.

External Validity

External validity is the extent to which the results can be generalized to the relevant populations, settings, treatments, or outcomes. Generally speaking, external validity can be secured if a true probability sampling technique (e.g., random selection) is utilized, although, logistically this is often extremely difficult. Therefore, it is feasible that cause and effect can be established via the application of a sound experiment, but the findings may not generalize to the appropriate population or settings. As seen in Table 1.2, the primary threats to external validity are detailed and primarily slanted toward the examinations of causal relationships. However, issues

Table 1.1 Threats to Internal Validity

Threat	Explanation
History	Any event that occurs during the time of the treatment and the posttest that could affect the outcome (e.g., natural life events such as a death in the family, change in job, or moving).
Maturation	The natural process of changing, growing, and learning over time.
Testing	The effects of practice familiarity in taking the same test more than once (e.g., the participant who takes the same math achievement test twice in the pretest and posttest measures may improve performance simply because of the familiarity with the test).
Instrumentation	The change in a measuring instrument over time (i.e., some instruments undergo revisions).
Statistical regression	The tendency for any extreme score to regress toward the average (i.e., regression toward the mean is a statistical phenomenon that any extreme scores, high or low, eventually regress or revert back to the average).
Selection bias	Also known as *selection effect*. Selection bias results when researchers do not use a systematic assignment technique (e.g., random assignment) to assign participants to conditions.
Attrition	The loss of participants during the term of the experiment.
Combination of selection and other treatments	Any one of the threats to internal validity can affect one of the groups in the study as opposed to the other (e.g., the participants in one condition may have been exposed to a stressful event not related to the experiment, but this event does not affect the other condition).
Diffusion	The inadvertent application of the treatment to the control group (e.g., in educational settings, teachers may utilize aspects of the math intervention in the control group that are supposed to be delivered only to the control condition).
Special treatment	The control group may receive special attention, and the changes may be attributed only to the attention (i.e., placebo effect).
Sequencing effects	Sequencing is an issue related to within-subject (repeated measures) approaches; also known as *multiple-treatment interference, fatigue effects,* and *practice effects.* Sequencing can be separated into *order effects* (i.e., the order in which participants receive the treatment can affect the results) and *carryover effects* (i.e., performance in one condition affects performance in another condition).

pertaining to external validity should be considered for nonexperimental research. The most obvious threat to external validity for survey approaches, for example, would be *sample characteristics,* sometimes referred to as *sampling bias.*

Table 1.2 Threats to External Validity

Threat	Explanation
Sample characteristics	The extent to which the sample (i.e., unit) represents the population from which it is drawn (i.e., for a sample to represent a population, the researcher must employ the appropriate sampling procedures and perform random selection).
Stimulus characteristics and settings	The unique factors involved in providing the treatment or intervention, such as the setting and researchers (i.e., it is difficult to replicate contrived laboratory conditions to real-life scenarios).
Treatment variations	Variations in the same treatment or the combination of multiple or partial treatments account for different results.
Outcome variations	Observing the effect of one type of outcome differs when alternate outcomes are observed.
Context-dependent mediation	Mediating variables related to outcomes differ between contexts or settings.

Construct Validity

Construct validity refers to the extent a generalization can be made from the operationalization (i.e., the scientific measurement) of the theoretical construct back to the conceptual basis responsible for the change in the outcome. Again, although the list of threats to construct validity seen in Table 1.3 are defined to imply issues regarding cause-effect relations, the premise of construct validity should apply to all types of research. Some authors categorize some of these threats as *social threats* to internal validity and some authors simply categorize some of the threats listed in Table 1.3 as threats to internal validity. The categorization of these threats can be debated, but the premise of the threats to validity cannot be argued (i.e., a violation of construct validity affects the overall validity of the study in the same way as a violation of internal validity).

Statistical Conclusion Validity

Statistical conclusion validity is the extent to which the statistical covariation (relationship) between the treatment and the outcome is accurate. Specifically, the statistical inferences regarding statistical conclusion validity has to do with the ability with which one can detect the relationship between the treatment and outcome, as well as determine the strength of the relationship between the two. As seen in Table 1.4, the most notable threats to statistical conclusion validity are outlined. Violating a threat to statistical conclusion validity typically will result in the overestimation or underestimation of the relationship between the treatment and outcome in experimental research. A violation can also result in the overestimation or underestimation of the explained or predicted relationships between variables as seen in nonexperimental research.

The reader is referred to the following books and article for an in-depth review of issues related to validity in research:

Cook, T. D., & Campbell, D. T. (1979). *Quasi-experimentation: Design and analysis issues for field settings.* Chicago, IL: Rand McNally.

Shadish, W. R. (2010). Campbell and Rubin: A primer and comparison of their approaches to causal inference in field settings. *Psychological Methods, 15,* 3–17.

Shadish, W. R., Cook, T. D., & Campbell, D. T. (2002). *Experimental and quasi-experimental designs for generalized causal inference.* Boston, MA: Houghton Mifflin.

DESIGN LOGIC ◆

As previously noted, the overarching objective of a research design is to provide a framework from which specific research questions or hypotheses can be answered while utilizing the scientific method. The concept of a research design and its structure is, at face value, rather simplistic. However, complexities arise when researchers apply research designs within social science paradigms. These include, but are not limited to, logistical issues, lack of control over certain variables, psychometric issues, and theoretical frameworks that are not well developed. In addition, as noted with statistical conclusion validity, a researcher can apply sound principles of scientific inquiry while applying an appropriate research design, but may compromise the findings with inappropriate statistical analyses. Shadish et al. (2002) emphasized the importance of structural design features and that researchers should focus on the theory of design logic as the most important feature in determining valid outcomes (or testing causal propositions). The logic of research designs is ultimately embedded within the scientific method, and applying the principles of sound scientific inquiry within this phase is of the utmost importance and the primary focus of this reference guide.

Table 1.3 Threats to Construct Validity

Threat	Explanation
Attention and contact with participants	Similar to *special treatment*, the level of attention, or differentiated attention, between the groups from the experimenter (e.g., the researcher spends more time with Group 1 than Group 2, and the differences observed in the outcome can be explained by the increased amount of attention and not due to the intervention).
Single operations and narrow stimulus sampling	The impact the researcher has on the development and implementation of the treatment (i.e., researchers deliver treatments differently based on experiences and expertise; therefore, it is difficult to measure the impact the researcher has on the treatment itself).
Experimenter expectancies	The researchers' expectancies, beliefs, and biases about the results (e.g., if a researcher strongly believes anxiety reduces test performance, then the interaction between the researcher and the participant may influence the outcome because the delivery of instructions and adherence to protocols may change).
Cues of the experimental situation	Sources of influence conveyed to prospective participants (e.g., rumors, information passed along from previous participants).
Novelty effects	The novelty of being in a new or innovative context.
Inadequate explication of constructs	The construct under investigation is not appropriately defined conceptually, which leads to inadequate measurement (i.e., operationalization).
Construct confounding	Multiple constructs are not clearly identified and accounted for operationally.
Mono-operation bias	An operationalization (i.e., measurement) that does not appropriately represent the construct under investigation which leads to measuring unintended constructs.
Mono-method bias	All measurement techniques are the same as a means to measure the construct under investigation.
Confounding constructs with levels of constructs	All the levels of a construct are not fully accounted for through the appropriate measurement and reporting tools.
Treatment sensitive factorial structure	The interpretation and structure of a measure changes as a result of the treatment.

Threat	Explanation
Reactivity to assessment	The participants' awareness of being studied may influence the outcome; also known as *acquiescence bias, social desirability,* and the *Hawthorne* or *Observer effect.* An unnatural reaction to any particular form of assessment (i.e., when participants know they are being assessed, the assessment is considered obtrusive and may alter outcome measures other than what they would naturally be).
Test sensitization	Also known as *pretest sensitization,* the sensitization to the intervention when participants are pretested (e.g., participants are pretested on perceptions of persuasive speeches and are then shown a movie on a persuasive speech; the pretest may influence how they view the speech).
Timing of measurement	The point in time the assessments are administered (i.e., unknown changes may occur, and the different timing of assessments may reveal different results).
Compensatory equalization	Participants in one condition receive more desirable services or compensation compared to that of another condition, thus constituents may provide enhanced services or goods to the condition not receiving the benefits.
Compensatory rivalry	Participants in the control condition make a concerted effort to make improvements or changes in line with the treatment condition.
Resentful demoralization	Participants become resentful or demoralized when they perceive they are receiving a less desirable treatment compared to that of another condition.

Control

Control is an important element to securing the validity of research designs within quantitative methods (i.e., experimental, quasi-experimental, and nonexperimental research). However, within qualitative methods, behavior is generally studied as it occurs naturally with no manipulation or control. Control refers to the concept of holding variables constant or systematically varying the conditions of variables based on theoretical considerations as a means to minimize the influence of unwanted variables (i.e., extraneous variables). Control can be applied actively within quantitative methods through (a) manipulation, (b) elimination, (c) inclusion, (d) group or condition assignment, or (e) statistical procedures.

In basic terms, *manipulation* is applied by manipulating (i.e., controlling) the independent variable(s). For example, a researcher can manipulate a behavioral intervention (i.e., independent variable) by systematically applying

Table 1.4 Threats to Statistical Conclusion Validity

Threat	Explanation
Low statistical power	Power is the extent to which the results of an analysis accurately reveal a statistically significant difference between groups (or cases) when a statistical difference truly exists.
Assumption violation of statistical tests	Violating the assumptions (depending on the extent of the violation) of statistical tests can lead to overestimation or underestimation of practical and statistical significance of an outcome.
Error rate problem	Statistical significance can be artificially inflated when performing multiple pairwise tests, also referred to as familywise error rate (i.e., the probability of making a Type I error when performing multiple pairwise analyses).
Restriction of range	Lack of variability between variables weakens the relationship and lowers statistical power.
Extraneous variance in the experimental setting	Variations within the experimental setting (e.g., temperature) may inflate error.
Inaccurate effect size estimation	Some statistical analyses can overestimate or underestimate the size of an effect.
Variability in the procedures	Also referred to as *unreliability of treatment implementation*, the variations in the application of an intervention may affect the outcome (i.e., a non-standardized approach will create variability in the outcome that is not attributable to the treatment, rather the application of the treatment).
Subject heterogeneity	The variability of participant demographics (e.g., age, race, ethnicity, background) may create unaccounted-for variations in the findings.
Unreliability of the measures	Measures maintain certain levels of validity and reliability (pertaining to psychometric principles), and lack of reliability causes inconsistency in measurement.
Multiple comparisons and error rates	The use of multiple dependent variables across conditions and multiple statistical analyses creates greater opportunities for error variance.

and removing the intervention or by controlling the frequency and duration of the application. *Elimination* is conducted when a researcher holds a variable or converts it to a constant. If, for example, a researcher ensures the temperature in a lab is set exactly to 76° Fahrenheit for both conditions in a biofeedback study, then the variable of temperature is eliminated as a factor because it is held as a constant. *Inclusion* refers to the addition of an extraneous variable into the design to test its affect on the outcome (i.e., dependent variable). For example, a researcher can include both males and females into a factorial design to examine the independent effects gender has on the outcome.

Inclusion can also refer to the addition of a control or comparison group within the research design. *Group assignment* is another major form of control (see more on group and condition assignments later). For the between-subjects approach, a researcher can exercise control through random assignment, utilizing a matching technique, or applying a cutoff score as means to assign participants to conditions. For the repeated-measures approach, control is exhibited when the researcher utilizes the technique of counterbalancing to variably expose each group or individual to all the levels of the independent variable. Last, the investigator can exhibit control using *statistical procedures* with variables, for example, by systematically deleting or not including cases and/or variables (i.e., removing outliers) within the analysis. As illustrated in Table 1.5, all of the major forms of control can be applied in the application of designs for experimental and quasi-experimental research. The only form of control that can be applied to nonexperimental research is statistical control.

Table 1.5 Control Techniques for Experimental, Quasi-Experimental, and Nonexperimental Research

Type of Control	Experimental and Quasi-Experimental Research	Nonexperimental Research
Manipulation	Yes	—
Elimination	Yes	—
Inclusion	Yes	—
Group or condition assignment	Yes	—
Statistical procedures	Yes	Yes

DESIGN NOTATIONS ♦

Design notations are the symbols used to diagrammatically illustrate the process of a research design (see Table 1.6). Within the design, time moves from left to right of the design structure. We utilized the design notations presented herein in each research design covered. The notations presented in this book are based on Campbell and Stanley's (1963) work.

Observation (O). Observation, also known as measurement, is symbolized by an "O." The O can refer to a single measure of the dependent variable or multiple measures ($O_1, O_2 \ldots O_n$).

Table 1.6 Design Notations

Design Notation	Design Element
O	Observation
X	Treatment
A, B	Factor

Treatment (X). Treatment, also known as intervention or program (i.e., the treatment is technically the independent variable and also referred to as a factor), is symbolized with an "X." A control group typically does not receive the treatment and is designated as "**-**" in its place.

Factor (A, B . . . Z). Multiple treatments (factors) utilized in a design are designated as "X_A" and "X_B" and can go as far up the alphabet as there are factors.

◆ ASSIGNMENT TECHNIQUES

In quantitative methods, each group in a research design has its own line within the structure of the diagram (see Table 1.7). One line equates to one group, two lines equate to two groups, and so on. The assignment of a group is usually the first design notation listed in the line structure.

Table 1.7 Group Assignment Design Notations

Design Notation	Assignment
R	Random
NR	Nonrandom
C	Cutoff score
M	Matched

Random assignment (R). Participants are randomly assigned to each condition to theoretically ensure group equivalency. Logistically, as seen in Figure 1.2, *stratified random assignment* (R_S), sometimes referred to as *blocking,* is used to ensure that the subjects are balanced within a predetermined stratum (e.g., age, ethnicity) and then randomly assigned to conditions.

Figure 1.2 Example of a Stratified Random Assignment Technique

	Sample of Subjects with GPAs ranging from 2.0 to 4.0 (N = 52)			
	Subjects with a GPA of 2.0 to 2.5 (n = 14)	Subjects with a GPA of 2.6 to 3.0 (n = 12)	Subjects with a GPA of 3.1 to 3.5 (n = 16)	Subjects with a GPA of 3.6 to 4.0 (n = 10)
	↓	↓	↓	↓
1 Treatment (×)	n = 7	n = 6	n = 8	n = 5
2 Control (–)	n = 7	n = 6	n = 8	n = 5

Note: This is an example of a two-group design (one treatment and one control group), and the pool of subjects is separated into strata based on grade point average (GPA; i.e., the stratification variable) and then randomly assigned to conditions. Some researchers recommend using this technique when N < 100 (Lachin, Matts, & Wei, 1988).

Nonrandom assignment (NR). Participants are assigned to each condition by a matter of convenience or necessity because random assignment is neither an option nor required (nonequivalent groups).

Cutoff score (C). A cutoff score (criterion) is used to assign participants to groups within regression-discontinuity approaches. To create a cutoff criterion, a single pretest continuous distribution is determined and then a division in the data (i.e., cutoff) is made that determines the assignment of participants to conditions.

Matched (M). Matching is a technique used by researchers to match participants on the basis of some extraneous variable that is related to the dependent variable. When this technique is used to assign participants to conditions, some researchers refer to these as match-group designs, but this is not entirely accurate. It is the assignment technique that changes, but the design remains the same.

> **Matched pairs.** For application in any research design indicated in the between-subjects approach, the researcher can (a) match participants in pairs based on certain criteria (e.g., IQ score), then randomly assign each member of the pair to conditions in order to ensure group equivalency (experimental design), and designate this as M_R; or (b) match participants based on certain criteria without random assignment to a specific group (quasi-experimental design), and designate this as M_{NR}. For more on matched pairs, see Shadish et al. (2002, p. 118).

> **Matched grouping.** For application in observational approaches, as well as the ex post facto (i.e., after the fact) design, the researcher manually matches participants in groups (M_A) as a means to establish control over the variables of interest. This is conducted because the independent [treatment] variable has already occurred and is not manipulated, therefore, various levels of alternate independent variables (e.g., age, gender) can be statistically manipulated and used as a means to assign individuals to conditions (see more on ex post facto designs later in this guide).

Counterbalancing. Counterbalancing is a technique used only in repeated-measures approaches to control for *sequencing effects.* Researchers utilize counterbalancing to variably expose each group or individual to all the treatments or various treatment levels. The most common form of counterbalancing is conducted at the group level (each group is exposed to the treatment at different sequences). However, counterbalancing can be randomized (sequence is randomly determined for each participant), intrasubject (participants are exposed to more than one sequence, usually in one order, then reversed), complete (every possible sequence is offered), or incomplete (not every sequence is provided because it would require too many conditions, as seen later in the Latin-square design).

The reader is referred to the following article and book for an in-depth review of topics related to group assignment:

Cook, T. D., & Steiner, P. M. (2010). Case matching and the reduction of selection bias in quasi-experiments: The relative importance of pretest measures of outcome, of unreliable measurement, and of mode of data analysis. *Psychological Methods, 15*(1), 56–68.

Rubin, D. B. (2006). *Matched sampling for causal effects.* Cambridge, England: Cambridge University Press.

♦ COMPARISON AND CONTROL GROUPS

The group that does not receive the actual treatment, or intervention, is typically designated as the control group. Control groups are comparison groups and are primarily used to address threats to internal validity such as history, maturation, selection, and testing. A *comparison group* refers to the group or groups that are not part of the primary focus of the investigation but allow the researcher to draw certain conclusions and strengthen aspects of internal validity. There are several distinctions and variations of the control group that should be clarified.

Control group. The control group, also known as the no-contact control, receives no treatment and no interaction.

Attention control group. The attention control group, also known as the attention-placebo, receives attention in the form of a pseudo-intervention to control for reactivity to assessment (i.e., the participant's awareness of being studied may influence the outcome).

Nonrandomly assigned control group. The nonrandomly assigned control is used when a no-treatment control group cannot be created through random assignment.

Wait-list control group. The wait-list control group is withheld from the treatment for a certain period of time, then the treatment is provided. The time in which the treatment is provided is based on theoretical tenets and on the pretest and posttest assessment of the original treatment group.

Historical control group. Historical control is a control group that is chosen from a group of participants who were observed at some time in the past or for whom data are available through archival records and sometimes referred to as *cohort* controls (i.e., a homogenous successive group) and are useful in quasi-experimental research.

SAMPLING STRATEGIES ♦

A major element to the logic of design extends to sampling strategies. When developing quantitative, qualitative, and mixed methods studies, it is important to identify the individuals (or extant databases) from whom you plan to collect data. To start, the *unit of analysis* must be indicated. The unit of analysis is the level or distinction of an entity that will be the focus of the study. Most commonly, in social science research, the unit of analysis is at the individual or group level, but it can also be at the programmatic level (e.g., institution or state level). There are instances when researchers identify a unit nested within an aggregated group (e.g., a portion of students within a classroom) and refer to this as *nested designs* or models. It should be noted that examining nested units is not a unique design, rather, a form of a sampling strategy, and the relevant aspects of statistical conclusion validity should be accounted for (e.g., independence assumptions). After identifying the unit, the next step is to identify the *population* (assuming the individual or group is the unit of analysis), which is the group of individuals who share similar characteristics (e.g., all astronauts). Logistically, it is impossible in most circumstances to collect data from an entire population; therefore, as illustrated in Figure 1.3, a *sample* (or subset) from the population is identified (e.g., astronauts who have completed a minimum of four human space-flight missions and work for NASA).

Figure 1.3 Example of a Sample Extracted From a Population

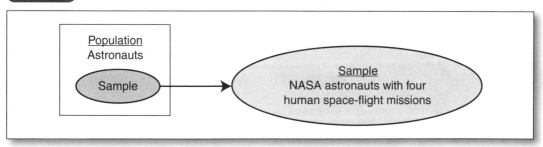

The goal is to eventually generalize the finding to the entire population. There are two major types of sampling strategies, probability and nonprobability sampling. In experimental, quasi-experimental, and nonexperimental (survey and observational) research, the focus should be on probability sampling (identifying and selecting individuals who are considered representative of the population). Many researchers also suggest that some form of probability sampling for observational (correlational) approaches (predictive designs) must be employed, otherwise the statistical outcomes cannot be generalizable. When it is not logistically possible to use probability sampling, or as seen in qualitative methods not necessary, some researchers utilize nonprobability sampling techniques (i.e., the researcher selects participants on a specific criterion and/or based on availability). The following list includes the major types of probability and nonprobability sampling techniques.

Probability Sampling Techniques

Simple random sampling. Every individual within the population has an equal chance of being selected.

Cluster sampling. Also known as area sampling, this allows the researcher to divide the population into clusters (based on regions) and then randomly select from the clusters.

Stratified sampling. The researcher divides the population in homogeneous subgroups (e.g., based on age) and then randomly selects participants from each subgroup.

Systematic sampling. Once the size of the sample is identified, the researcher selects every nth individual (e.g., every third person on the list of participants is selected) until the desired sample size is fulfilled.

Multistage sampling. The researcher combines any of the probability sampling techniques as a means to randomly select individuals from the population.

Nonprobability Sampling Techniques

Convenience sampling. Sometimes referred to as haphazard or accidental sampling, the investigator selects individuals because they are available and willing to participate.

Purposive sampling. The researcher selects individuals to participate based on a specific need or purpose (i.e., based on the research objective, design, and target population); this is most commonly used for qualitative methods (see Patton, 2002). Variations of purposive sampling include *snowball, expert,* and *heterogeneity* sampling. *Theoretical* sampling is a type of purposive sampling utilized in grounded-theory approaches.

The reader is referred to the following book for an in-depth review of a topic related to sampling strategies for quantitative and qualitative methods:

Levy, P. S., & Lemeshow, S. (2009). *Sampling of populations: Methods and applications* (4th ed.). New York, NY: John Wiley & Sons.

PART I

Quantitative Methods for Experimental and Quasi-Experimental Research

T his Part includes four popular approaches to the quantitative method (experimental and quasi-experimental only), followed by some of the associated basic designs (accompanied by brief descriptions of published studies that utilized the design). For an in-depth understanding of the application of the design, the full article can be reviewed on the companion website, *A Cross-Section of Research Articles Classified by Design: Quantitative, Qualitative, and Mixed Methods* (http://www.sagepub.com/edmonds).

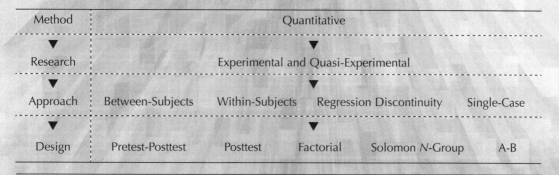

Method	Quantitative				
▼			▼		
Research	Experimental and Quasi-Experimental				
▼			▼		
Approach	Between-Subjects	Within-Subjects	Regression Discontinuity		Single-Case
▼			▼		
Design	Pretest-Posttest	Posttest	Factorial	Solomon *N*-Group	A-B

Note: Quantitative methods for experimental and quasi-experimental research are shown here, followed by the approach and then the design.

Research in quantitative methods essentially refers to the application of the systematic steps of the scientific method, while utilizing quantitative properties (i.e., numerical systems) to research the relationships or effects of specific variables. Measurement is the critical component of the quantitative method. Measurement reveals and illustrates the relationship between quantitatively derived variables. Variables within quantitative methods must be, first, conceptually defined (i.e., the scientific definition), then operationalized (i.e., determine the appropriate measurement tool based on the conceptual definition). Research in quantitative methods is typically referred to as a deductive process and iterative in nature. That is, based on the findings, a theory is supported (or not), expanded, or refined and further tested.

Researchers must employ the following steps when determining the appropriate quantitative research design. First, a measurable or testable research question (or hypothesis) must be formulated. The question must maintain the following qualities: (a) precision, (b) viability, and (c) relevance. The question must be *precise* and well formulated. The more precise the easier it is to appropriately operationalize the variables of interest. The question must be *viable* in that it is logistically feasible or plausible to collect data on the variable(s) of interest. The question must also be *relevant* so that the result of the findings will maintain an appropriate level of practical and scientific meaning. The second step includes choosing the appropriate design based on the primary research question, the variables of interest, and logistical considerations. The researcher must also determine if randomization to conditions is possible or plausible. In addition, decisions must be made about how and where the data will be collected. The design will assist in determining when the data will be collected. The unit of analysis (i.e., individual, group, or program level), population, sample, and sampling procedures should be identified in this step. Third, the variables must be operationalized. And last, the data are collected following the format of the framework provided by the research design of choice.

♦ EXPERIMENTAL RESEARCH

Experimental research (sometimes referred to as randomized experiments or randomized control trials) is considered to be the most powerful type of research in determining causation among variables. Cook and Campbell (1979) presented three conditions that must be met in order to establish cause and effect: (a) covariation (the change in the cause must be related to the effect), (b) temporal precedence (the cause must precede the effect), and (c) no plausible alternative explanations (the cause must be the only explanation for the effect). The essential features of experimental research are the sound application of the elements of control: (a) manipulation, (b) elimination, (c) inclusion, (d) group or condition assignment, or (e) statistical procedures. Random assignment (not to be confused with random selection) of participants to conditions (or random assignment of conditions to participants [counterbalancing] as seen in repeated-measures approaches) is a critical step, which allows for increased control (improved internal validity) and limits the impact of the confounding effects of variables that are not being studied. The random assignment to each group (condition) theoretically ensures that the groups are "probabilistically" equivalent (controlling for selection bias), and any differences observed in the pretests (if collected) are considered due to chance. Therefore, if all threats to internal, external, construct, and statistical conclusion validity were secured at "adequate" levels (i.e., all plausible alternative explanations are accounted for), the differences observed in the posttest measures can be attributed fully to the experimental treatment (i.e., cause and effect can be established). Conceptually, a causal effect is defined as a comparison of outcomes derived from treatment and control conditions on a common set of units (e.g., school, person).

The strength of experimental research rests in the reduction of threats to internal validity. Many threats are controlled for through the application of random assignment of participants to conditions. *Random selection,* on the other hand, is related to sampling procedures and is a major factor in establishing external validity (i.e., generalizability of results). Randomly selecting a sample from a population would be conducted so that the sample would better represent the population. Random assignment is related to design and random selection is related to sampling procedures. Shadish et al. (2002) introduced the term *generalized causal inference.* They posit that, if a researcher follows the appropriate tenets of experimental design logic (e.g., includes the appropriate number of subjects, utilizes random selection and random assignment) and controls for threats of all types of validity (including test validity), then valid causal inferences can be determined along with the ability to generalize the causal link. This is truly realized once multiple replications of the experiment are conducted and comparable results can be observed over time (replication being the operative word). To be more specific, although probability sampling (e.g., random selection) adds another logistical obstacle to experimental research, it should also be an emphasis along with the proper random assignment techniques.

♦ QUASI-EXPERIMENTAL RESEARCH

The nonrandom assignment of participants to each condition allows for convenience when it is logistically not possible to utilize random assignment. Quasi-experimental research designs are also referred to as field research (i.e., research is conducted with an intact group in the field as opposed to the lab), and they are also known as nonequivalent designs (i.e., participants are not randomly assigned to each condition; therefore, the groups are assumed nonequivalent). Hence, the major difference between experimental and quasi-experimental research designs is the level of control and assignment to conditions. The actual designs are structurally the same, but the analyses of the data are not. However, some of the basic pretest and posttest designs can be modified (e.g., addition of multiple observations or inclusion of comparison groups) in an attempt to compensate for lack of group equivalency. In the design structure, a dashed line (- - -) between groups indicates the participants were not randomly assigned to conditions. Review Appendix A for more examples of "quasi-experimental" research designs (see also example of diagram that follows).

Because there is no random assignment in quasi-experimental research, there may be confounding variables influencing the outcome not fully attributed to the treatment (i.e., causal inferences drawn from quasi-experiments must be made with extreme caution). The pretest measure in quasi-experimental research allows the researcher to evaluate the lack of group equivalency and selection bias, thus altering the statistical analysis between experimental and quasi-experimental research for the exact same design (see Cribbie, Arpin-Cribbie, & Gruman, 2010, for a discussion on tests of equivalence for independent group designs with more than two groups).

Group	Assignment	Pretest	Pretest	Treatment	Posttest
1	NR	O_1	O_2	X	O_3
2	NR	O_1	O_2	—	O_3

Time ▶

Note: This is an example of a between-subjects approach with a double pretest design. The double pretest allows the researcher to compare the "treatment effects" between O_1 to O_2, and then from O_2 to O_3. A major threat to internal validity with this design is testing, but it controls for selection bias and maturation. The two pretests are not necessary if random assignment is utilized.

It is not recommended to utilize posttest-only designs for quasi-experimental research. However, if theoretically or logistically it does not make sense to utilize a pretest measure, then additional controls should be implemented, such as using historical control groups, proxy pretest variables (see Appendix A), or the matching technique to assign participants to conditions. The reader is referred to Shadish, Clark, and Steiner (2008) for an in-depth discussion of the potential weaknesses and strengths of quasi-experimental research in determining causation.

CHAPTER **2**

BETWEEN-SUBJECTS APPROACH

The between-subjects approach, also known as a multiple-group approach, allows a researcher to compare the effects of two or more groups on single or multiple dependent variables (outcome variables). With a minimum of two groups, the participants in each group will only be exposed to one condition (one level of the independent variable), with no crossover between conditions. An advantage of having multiple groups is that it allows for the (a) random assignment to different conditions (experimental research) and (b) comparison of different treatments. If the design includes two or more dependent variables, it can be referred to as a multivariate approach, and when the design includes one dependent variable, it is classified as univariate.

◆ PRETEST AND POSTTEST DESIGNS

A common application to experimental and quasi-experimental research is the pretest and posttest between-subjects approach, also referred to as an Analysis of Covariance Design (i.e., the pretest measure is used as the *covariate* in the analyses because the pretest should be highly correlated with the posttest). The 1-factor pretest and posttest control group design is one of the most common between-subjects approaches with many variations (one factor representing one independent variable and sometimes referred to as a single-factor randomized-group design). This basic multiple-group design can include a control group and is designed to have multiple measures between and within groups. Although there is a within-subject component, the emphasis is on the between-subject variance. The advantage of including pretest measures allows for the researcher to test for group equivalency (i.e., homogeneity between groups) and for providing a baseline against which to compare the treatment effects, which is the within-subject component of the design (i.e., the pretest is designated as the covariate in order to assess the variance [distance between each set of data points] between the pretest and posttest measures).

There is no set rule that determines the number of observations that should be made on the dependent variable. For example, in a basic pretest and posttest control group design, an observation is taken once prior to the treatment and once after the treatment. However, based on theoretical considerations, the investigator can take multiple posttest treatment measures by including a time-series component. Depending on the research logistics, groups can be randomly assigned or matched, then randomly assigned to meet the criteria for experimental research, or groups can be nonrandomly assigned to conditions (quasi-experimental research). With quasi-experimental research, the limitations of the study significantly increase as defined by the threats to internal validity discussed earlier.

k-Factor Designs

The between-subjects approach can include more than one treatment (factor) or intervention (i.e., the independent variable) and does not always have to include a control group. We designate this design as the *k*-factor design, with or without a control group. Shadish et al. (2002) refer to this design as an alternative- or multiple-treatment design. We prefer the *k*-factor design as a means to clearly distinguish exactly how many factors are present in the design (i.e., the *k* represents the number of factors [independent variables]). To clarify, the treatments in a 3-factor model ($k = 3$), for example, would be designated as X_A, X_B, and X_C (each letter of the alphabet representing a factor) within the design structure. The within-subjects *k*-factor design is referred to as the cross-over design and is discussed in more detail later in this book under repeated-measures approaches.

A between-subjects *k*-factor design should be used when a researcher wants to examine the effectiveness of more than one type of treatment and a true control is not feasible. Within educational settings, a control group is sometimes not accessible, or there are times when a university's Institutional Review Board considers the withholding of treatment from specific populations as unethical. Furthermore, some psychologists and educators believe that using another treatment (intervention) as a comparison group will yield more meaningful results, particularly when the types of interventions being studied have a history of proven success; therefore, a *k*-factor design is the obvious choice. We present a variety of examples of 2-, 3-, and 4-factor pretest and posttest designs, as well as posttest-only designs with and without control groups.

Most common threats to internal validity are related, but not limited, to these designs:

> *Experimental:* Maturation, Testing, Attrition, History, and Instrumentation

> *Quasi-Experimental:* Maturation, Testing, Instrumentation, Attrition, History, and Selection Bias

The reader is referred to the following article and book for full explanations regarding threats to validity, grouping, and research designs:

> Shadish, W. R., & Cook, T. D. (2009). The renaissance of field experimentation in evaluating interventions. *The Annual Review of Psychology, 60,* 607–629.

> Shadish, W. R., Cook, T. D., & Campbell, D. T. (2002). *Experimental and quasi-experimental designs for generalized causal inference.* Boston, MA: Houghton Mifflin.

Example for Diagram 2.1

Chao, P., Bryan, T., Burstein, K., & Ergul, C. (2006). Family-centered intervention for young children at-risk for language and behavior problems. *Early Childhood Education Journal, 34*(2), 147–153.

Research Question: Does active parent engagement in selecting and using routine-based activities have a positive effect on children's language and appropriate behavior development?

Procedures: The researchers randomly assigned parents to a control and an intervention group. The control group included parents of 19 children, and the intervention group consisted of parents of 22 children. Children in the

Diagram 2.1 Pretest and Posttest Control Group Design

Group	Pretest	Treatment	Posttest
1	O_1	X	O_2
2	O_1	—	O_2

Time ▶

Note: In regard to design notations, a dashed line (- - -) would separate groups 1 and 2 in the design structure if the participants were not randomly assigned to conditions, which indicates quasi-experimental research.

control group participated only in the pretesting and posttesting phases of the study. Their parents did not receive training and were not required to attend regular meetings or submit weekly and monthly assessments of their children. Parents of children in the family-centered intervention group were trained to use the Child Behavior and Language Assessment (CBLA). Both groups were pretested and posttested on the Test of Early Language Development-Third Edition (TELD-3) and the Eyberg Child Behavior Inventory (ECBI).

Design: Experimental research utilizing a between-subjects approach with a pre- and posttest control group design

Recommended parametric analysis: Analysis of Covariance (ANCOVA), Multivariate Analysis of Covariance (MANCOVA), two-way Repeated Measures Analysis of Variance (RM-ANOVA), or two-way Repeated Measures Multivariate Analysis of Variance (RM-MANOVA; appropriate descriptive statistics and effect-size calculations should be included).

Assignment	Group	Pretest	Treatment	Posttest
R	1 ($n = 22$)	TELD-3, ECBI	Family-centered intervention	TELD-3, ECBI
R	2 ($n = 19$)	TELD-3, ECBI	—	TELD-3, ECBI
		Time ▶		

Diagram 2.2 2-Factor Pretest and Posttest Control Group Design

Group	Pretest	Treatment	Posttest
1	O_1	X_A	O_2
2	O_1	X_B	O_2
3	O_1	—	O_2

Time ▶

Example for Diagram 2.2

Kazdin, A. E., Esveldt-Dawson, K., French, N. H., & Unis, A. S. (1987). Problem-solving skills training and relationship therapy in the treatment of antisocial child behavior. *Journal of Counseling and Clinical Psychology,* *55*(1), 76–85.

Research Question: What are the effects of cognitive-behavioral problem-solving skills training and nondirective relationship therapy on antisocial child behavior?

Procedures: Children were randomly assigned to one of three conditions: (a) problem-solving skills training, (b) relationship therapy, or (c) a treatment-control group. The children met individually for 20 sessions in the two treatment conditions. Sessions lasted approximately 45 minutes and were administered two to three times per week. Treatments were completed while the children were in the hospital. After completion of the sessions, the children were discharged. A treatment-control group was used to partially control for therapist contact and attendance at special sessions outside of the usual ward routine. Children were assessed before and after the intervention with the Child Behavior Checklist (CBCL) and the School Behavior Checklist (SBCL).

Design: Experimental research utilizing a between-subjects approach with a 2-factor pretest and posttest control group design

Recommended parametric analysis: ANCOVA, MANCOVA, two-way RM-ANOVA, or two-way RM-MANOVA (appropriate descriptive statistics and effect-size calculations should be included).

Assignment	Group	Pretest	Treatment	Posttest
R	1 (*n* = 20)	CBCL, SBCL	Problem solving	CBCL, SBCL
R	2 (*n* = 19)	CBCL, SBCL	Relationship therapy	CBCL, SBCL
R	3 (*n* = 17)	CBCL, SBCL	—	CBCL, SBCL
Time ▶				

Diagram 2.3 2-Factor Pretest and Posttest Design

Group	Pretest	Treatment	Posttest
1	O_1	X_A	O_2
2	O_1	X_B	O_2

Time ▶

Example for Diagram 2.3

Comaskey, E. M., Savage, R. S., & Abrami, P. (2009). A randomized efficacy study of web-based synthetic and analytic programmes among disadvantaged urban kindergarten children. *Journal of Research in Reading, 32*(1), 92–108.

Research Question: Does the ABRACADABRA literacy program produce different effects for synthetic and analytic phonics interventions on phonological, word, and nonword measures?

Procedures: Children were randomly assigned to either the synthetic or analytic phonics intervention group using a manual random-allocation process (allocation cards pulled blind from a hat). This resulted in 27 participants in the analytic phonics group and 26 participants in the synthetic phonics group. Students were engaged in other learning centers and would rotate into the "ABRA" center during the designated time periods. Children would engage in ABRA activities around a single computer supported by a facilitator. Interventions for the synthetic and analytic phonics groups followed the same lesson structure, beginning with an Animated Alphabet followed by a "core activity." Three major measures were used in the pretesting and posttesting sessions, which were the Peabody Picture Vocabulary Test (PPVT) vocabulary scale, Letter-Sound Knowledge (L-SK), and the Wide Range Achievement Test (WRAT).

Design: Experimental research utilizing a between-subjects approach with a 2-factor pretest and posttest design

Recommended parametric analysis: ANCOVA, MANCOVA, two-way RM-ANOVA, or two-way RM-MANOVA (appropriate descriptive statistics and effect-size calculations should be included).

Assignment	Group	Pretest	Treatment	Posttest
R	1 ($n = 27$)	PPVT, L-SK, WRAT	Synthetic Phonics	PPVT, L-SK, WRAT
R	2 ($n = 26$)	PPVT, L-SK, WRAT	Analytic Phonics	PPVT, L-SK, WRAT
Time ▶				

Diagram 2.4 3-Factor Pretest and Posttest Design

Group	Pretest	Treatment	Posttest
1	O_1	X_A	O_2
2	O_1	X_B	O_2
3	O_1	X_C	O_2

Time ▶

Example for Diagram 2.4

Lee, Y., Park, S., Kim, M., Son, C., & Lee, M. (2005). The effects of visual illustrations on learners' achievement and interest in PDA- (personal digital assistant) based learning. *Journal of Educational Computing Research, 33*(2), 173–187.

Research Question: What are the effects of three types of visual illustrations on learners' achievements, interests, and time spent reading content-specific materials?

Procedures: Participants were randomly assigned to one of three treatment groups: the cognitive interest illustration group, the emotional interest illustration group, and the text-only group. The instructional material containing cognitive interest illustrations consisted of a PDA-based presentation on the topic of the life cycle of the hurricane. Each participant was given the material corresponding to his or her treatment group. A multiple-choice test was used to measure pretest and posttest interest on the topic. Participants then received posttest assessments on achievement and time spent reading the materials.

Design: Experimental research utilizing a between-subjects approach with a 3-factor pretest and posttest design

Recommended parametric analysis: ANCOVA, MANCOVA, two-way RM-ANOVA, or two-way RM-MANOVA (appropriate descriptive statistics and effect-size calculations should be included).

Assignment	Group	Pretest	Treatment	Posttest
R	1 ($n = 15$)	Interest	Cognitive interest	Interest, achievement, time on reading
R	2 ($n = 15$)	Interest	Emotional interest	Interest, achievement, time on reading
R	3 ($n = 15$)	Interest	Text-only	Interest, achievement, time on reading
		Time ▶		

Diagram 2.5 4-Factor Pretest and Posttest Design

Group	Pretest	Treatment	Posttest
1	O_1	X_A	O_2
2	O_1	X_B	O_2
3	O_1	X_C	O_2
4	O_1	X_D	O_2

Time ▶

Example for Diagram 2.5

Kramarski, B., & Mevarech, Z. R. (2003). Enhancing mathematical reasoning in the classroom: The effects of cooperative learning and metacognitive training. *American Educational Research Journal, 40*(1), 281–310.

Research Question: What are the effects of cooperative learning strategies with and without metacognitive training, and individualized learning strategies with and without metacognitive training, on mathematical reasoning and metacognitive knowledge?

Procedures: Four schools ($N = 384$) were randomly assigned from a pool of 15 schools to one of four treatment conditions: (a) cooperative learning with metacognitive training (COOP+META), (b) cooperative learning (COOP), (c) individualized learning with metacognitive training (IND+META), and (d) individualized learning. All groups received math instruction five times per week with the difference between the groups being the instructional method. The COOP+META condition studied in small heterogeneous groups using metacognitive strategies. The IND+META condition was the same as the first condition, but students studied individually as opposed to groups. The COOP condition studied in heterogeneous groups but did not use metacognitive training, while the IND group studied individually with no metacognitive training. All groups were administered a graph interpretation test, graph construction test, and a metacognitive questionnaire before and after the completion of the study.

Design: Experimental research utilizing a between-subjects approach with a 4-factor pretest and posttest design

Recommended parametric analysis: ANCOVA, MANCOVA, two-way RM-ANOVA, or two-way RM-MANOVA (appropriate descriptive statistics and effect-size calculations should be included).

◆ POSTTEST DESIGNS

Another approach to experimental research is the between-subjects (or multiple-group) approach, posttest design. The two-group posttest control group design is one of the more common approaches within this structure. By removing the pretest observation, the within-subject component is eliminated. The main idea behind collecting pretest measures is to ensure

Assignment	Group	Pretest	Treatment	Posttest
R	1 (*n* = 105)	Graph interpretation and construction, metacognitive questionnaire	COOP+META	Graph interpretation and construction, metacognitive questionnaire
R	2 (*n* = 95)	Graph interpretation and construction, metacognitive questionnaire	IND+META	Graph interpretation and construction, metacognitive questionnaire
R	3 (*n* = 91)	Graph interpretation and construction, metacognitive questionnaire	COOP	Graph interpretation and construction, metacognitive questionnaire
R	4 (*n* = 93)	Graph interpretation and construction, metacognitive questionnaire	IND	Graph interpretation and construction, metacognitive questionnaire
Time ▶				

group equivalency and control for selection bias, but it also allows for the examination of the differences between baseline (pretest) and posttest measures following the treatment. With posttest-only designs, if random assignment is utilized, then group equivalency is "secured." Because only one posttest is observed per condition, this design is not the most rigorous (due to the lack of comparative observations); however, in terms of internal validity, the two-group posttest control group design is considered one of the strongest.

Research in education does not always allow for conditions suitable for random assignment; therefore, posttest-only designs are not recommended, but they are sometimes the only viable option. Therefore, if random assignment is not used, then a cohort matching technique (i.e., homogeneous groups are assigned to conditions, such as participants from the same class) should be used to assign participants to conditions. The design presented in Diagram 2.6 is a strong alternative for researchers within the field of education who typically cannot utilize random assignment but have access to groups considered as cohorts. The design includes a between-subjects component and combines a historical-control group with a one-group posttest-only design. For example, the researcher can match a group by grade level (i.e., cohort) and then assess the effects of a treatment by contrasting the differences between O_1 of the control and O_1 of the treatment group. An example of the use of this design might include accessing scores on a standardized achievement test (Group 1: O_1) of last year's seniors with the current senior class's scores (Group 2: O_1), but only after they received an educational specific intervention (X). Group 1 is designated as a *historical* cohort (i.e., homogeneous) control group.

Diagram 2.6		Example of a Posttest Only and a Historical Control Group Design		
Group	Assignment	Test	Treatment	Posttest
1	NR	O_1	—	—
2	NR	—	X	O_1

Time ▶

Note: This design would be designated as quasi-experimental research. History would be the biggest threat to internal validity. An independent-samples *t* test is the appropriate analysis for this design.

Most common threats to internal validity are related, but not limited, to these designs:

Experimental: Generally, all threats to internal validity are adequately controlled for.

Quasi-Experimental: History, Maturation, Statistical Regression, and Selection Bias

Diagram 2.7	Posttest Control Group Design	
Group	Treatment	Posttest
1	X	O_1
2	—	O_1

Time ▶

Example for Diagram 2.7

Dennis, J. K. (2003). Problem-based learning in online vs. face-to-face environments. *Education for Health, 16*(2), 198–209.

Research Question: What are the differences between online and traditional problem-based learning programs?

Procedures: Students were randomly assigned to one of two conditions: computer-mediated or control (i.e., traditional face-to-face). Students generated learning issues during the initial modules. The students then researched their learning issues and returned with their findings for the second tutorials. Students in the computer-mediated groups interacted with the resource person via e-mail, chat room, or bulletin board only. Following the training, posttest data was collected on learning outcomes (measured by a course examination), time on task (the self-reported time spent in and out of class on learning activities), and generation of learning issues.

Design: Experimental research utilizing a between-subjects approach with a posttest control group design

Recommended parametric analysis: Independent-samples *t* test, ANOVA, or MANOVA (appropriate descriptive statistics and effect-size calculations should be included).

Assignment	Group	Treatment	Posttest
R	1 (*n* = 17)	Computer-mediated problem-based learning	Learning outcomes, time on task, learning issues
R	2 (*n* = 17)	—	Learning outcomes, time on task, learning issues
		Time ▶	

Diagram 2.8 2-Factor Posttest Control Group Design

Group	Treatment	Posttest
1	X_A	O_1
2	X_B	O_1
3	—	O_1
	Time ▶	

Example for Diagram 2.8

Green, M., & Cifuentes, L. (2008). An exploration of online environments supporting follow-up to face-to-face professional development. *Journal of Technology and Teacher Education, 16*(3), 283–306.

Research Question: To what extent do participants' attitudes and course completion rates of online teacher professional-development programs differ based on the type of training program?

Procedures: Prior to the assignment to each condition, participants were blocked into strata based on service and socioeconomic status (SES). Participants were then randomly assigned (stratified random assignment) to one of three conditions: (a) follow-up with peer interaction, (b) follow-up without peer interaction, and (c) control condition (i.e., traditional training). Each condition included training using the WebCT platform. The two treatment conditions were developed based on the Texas Assessment of Knowledge and Skills standards. The peer-interaction group interacted on a weekly basis based on the content from relevant journal articles, websites, and Microsoft PowerPoint, whereas the other group did not interact. All three conditions were administered a posttest assessment on the attitude of the training modules; completion rates of the workshops were also recorded.

Design: Experimental research utilizing a between-subjects approach with a 2-factor posttest control group design

Recommended parametric analysis: ANOVA, or MANOVA (appropriate descriptive statistics and effect-size calculations should be included).

Assignment	Group	Treatment	Posttest
R_s	1 ($n = 94$)	Follow-up with peer interaction	Attitude survey, course completion
R_s	2 ($n = 98$)	Follow-up without peer interaction	Attitude survey, course completion
R_s	3 ($n = 88$)	—	Attitude survey, course completion
Time ▶			

| Diagram 2.9 | 2-Factor Posttest Design |

Group	Treatment	Posttest
1	X_A	O_1
2	X_B	O_1

Time ▶

Example for Diagram 2.9

Villalta-Gil, V., Roca, M., Gonzales, N., Domènec, E., Cuca, Escanilla, A., . . . Haro, J. M. (2009). Dog-assisted therapy in the treatment of chronic schizophrenia inpatients. *Antrozoös, 22*(2), 149–159.

Research Question: Does dog-assisted therapy improve the perceptions of social competence, quality of life, negative and positive symptoms, and satisfaction of schizophrenia inpatients?

Procedures: Patients diagnosed with schizophrenia living in long-term care units were randomly assigned to one of two treatment conditions: Integrated Psychological Treatment ($n = 9$) and Integrated Psychological Treatment with a therapy dog ($n = 12$). The treatment intervention included 25 sessions of 45 minutes each following the Integrated Psychological Treatment guidelines. A certified female Labrador therapy dog was used to assist the psychologist with the dog-therapy condition. Posttests were administered following the intervention and included the Positive and Negative Symptoms scale, the Living Skills scale, the Brief World Health Organization Quality of Life assessment, and a satisfaction with treatment scale.

Design: Experimental research utilizing a between-subjects approach with a 2-factor posttest design

Recommended parametric analysis: independent-samples *t* test, ANOVA, or MANOVA (appropriate descriptive statistics and effect-size calculations should be included).

Example for Diagram 2.10

Stewart, A. L., King, A. C., & Haskell, W. L. (1993). Endurance exercise and health-related quality of life in 50-65 year-old adults. *The Gerontologist, 33*(6), 782–789.

Assignment	Group	Treatment	Posttest
R	1 ($n = 12$)	Integrated Psychological Treatment with therapy dog	Positive and Negative Symptoms scale, Living Skills Profile, quality of life, satisfaction
R	2 ($n = 9$)	Integrated Psychological Treatment	Positive and Negative Symptoms scale, Living Skills Profile, quality of life, satisfaction
		Time ▶	

Diagram 2.10 3-Factor Posttest Design

Group	Treatment	Posttest
1	X_A	O_1
2	X_B	O_1
3	X_C	O_1

Time ▶

Research Question: What are the differences between group-based high intensity training, home-based high intensity training, and home-based low intensity training on the VO_2 max, body mass index (BMI), and quality of life indicators of older adults?

Procedures: One hundred and ninety-four participants were randomly assigned to one of three conditions: (a) group-based high intensity training, (b) home-based high intensity training, and (c) home-based low intensity training. The group-based sessions were conducted at a local community college. The home-based training included a first-time face-to-face session and subsequent weekly phone calls for the first four weeks, biweekly for the following four weeks, and then once a month for the remainder of the 12-month program. Following the yearlong program, participants' VO_2 max, BMI, and perceptions of quality of life were assessed.

Design: Experimental research utilizing a between-subjects approach with a 3-factor posttest design

Recommended parametric analysis: ANOVA or MANOVA (appropriate descriptive statistics and effect-size calculations should be included).

CHAPTER 3

REGRESSION-DISCONTINUITY APPROACH

The regression-discontinuity (RD) approach is often referred to as an RD design. RD approaches maintain the same design structure as any basic between-subjects pretest and posttest design. The major differences for the RD approach are (a) the method by which research participants are assigned to conditions and (b) the statistical analyses used to test the effects. Specifically, the researcher applies the RD approach as a means of assigning participants to conditions within the design structure by utilizing a cutoff score (criterion) on a predetermined quantitative measure (usually the dependent variable, but not always). Theoretical and logistical considerations are used to determine the cutoff criterion. The cutoff criterion is considered an advantage over typical random or nonrandom assignment approaches as a means to target "needy" participants and assign them to the actual program or treatment condition.

The most basic design utilized in RD approaches is the two-group pretest-posttest control group design. However, most designs designated as between-subject approaches can utilize a RD approach as a method of assignment to conditions and subsequent regression analysis. RD approaches can also be applied utilizing data from extant databases (e.g., Luytena, Tymms, & Jones, 2009) as a means to infer causality without designing a true randomized experiment (see also Lesik, 2006, 2008). As seen in the Figure 3.1, the cutoff criterion was 50 (based on a composite rating of 38 to 62). Those who scored below 50 were assigned to the control group and those who scored above were assigned to the treatment group. As seen in the figure, once the posttest scores were collected, a regression line is applied to the model to analyze the pre-post score relationship (i.e., a treatment effect is determined by assessing the degree of change in the regression line in observed and predicted pre-post scores for those who received treatment compared to those who did not). Some researchers argue that the RD approach does not compromise internal validity to the extent the findings would not be robust to any violations of assumptions (statistically speaking). Typically, an RD approach requires much larger samples as a means to achieve acceptable levels of power (see statistical conclusion validity). We present two examples of studies that utilized RD approaches: one that implemented an intervention and one that utilized observational data. See Shadish, Cook, and Campbell (2002) for an in-depth discussion of issues related to internal validity for RD approaches, as well as methods for classifying RD approaches as experimental research, quasi-experimental research, and fuzzy regression discontinuity (i.e., assigning participants to conditions in violation of the designated cutoff score).

Most common threats to internal validity are related, but not limited, to these designs:

Experimental. History, Maturation, and Instrumentation

Quasi-Experimental. History, Maturation, Instrumentation, and Selection Bias

Figure 3.1   Sample of a Cutoff Score

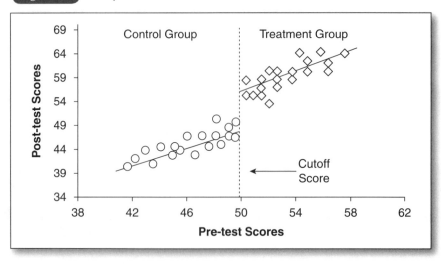

The reader is referred to the following articles and book chapter for full explanations regarding RD approaches:

Imbens, G. W., & Lemieux, T. (2008). Regression discontinuity designs: A guide to practice. *Journal of Econometrics, 142,* 615–635.

Trochim, W. (2001). Regression-discontinuity design. In N. J. Smelser, J. D. Wright, & P. B. Baltes (Eds.), *International encyclopedia of the social and behavioral sciences* (Vol. 19, pp. 12940–12945). North-Holland, Amsterdam: Pergamon.

Trochim, W., & Cappelleri, J. C. (1992). Cutoff assignment strategies for enhancing randomized clinical trials. *Controlled Clinical Trials, 13,* 190–212.

Diagram 3.1 Regression-Discontinuity Pretest-Posttest Control Group Design[1]

Pretest	Assignment	Group	Treatment	Posttest
O_A	C	1	X	O_2
O_A	C	2	—	O_2

Time ▶

Note: O_A refers to the preassignment measure and C refers to the cutoff score.

Example for Diagram 3.1

Bryant, D. P., Bryant, B. R., Gersten, R., Scammacca, N., & Chavez, M. M. (2008). Mathematic intervention for first- and second-grade students with mathematics difficulties: The effects of tier 2 intervention delivered at booster lessons. *Remedial and Special Education, 29*(1), 20–31.

Research Question: What are the effects of a Tier 2 mathematical intervention on mathematical achievement of first- and second-grade students?

Procedures: The effects of the intervention were determined by including a total of 126 first graders and 140 second graders from a primary-level elementary school. The students were then assessed using the Texas Early

Mathematics Inventory-Progress Monitoring (TEMI-PM). Based on the initial results, students who scored at or below the 25th percentile (standard score of 90 or below) were assigned as Tier 2 and subsequently were assigned to the treatment condition. Students who scored above 90 were assigned to the control condition. The result of the cutoff criterion was 26 first graders and 25 second graders who qualified for Tier 2, which included the intervention. The intervention was conceptualized as a booster or supplement to their regular course instruction. This included being exposed to 18 weeks of tutoring sessions. The intervention was grounded in the Texas Essential Knowledge and Skills (TEKS) standards. After the completion of the intervention all students were administered the TEMI-PM.

Design: Experimental research utilizing a RD approach with a pretest-posttest control group design

Recommended parametric analysis: See Imbens and Lemieux (2008) for details.

Pretest	Assignment	Group	Treatment	Posttest
TEMI-PM	C	1 ($n = 51$)	TEKS	TEMI-PM
TEMI-PM	C	2 ($n = 215$)	—	TEMI-PM
Time ▶				

Note: Group = first and second graders.

| **Diagram 3.2** | Regression-Discontinuity Pretest-Posttest Control Group Design[2] |

Pretest	Assignment	Group	Treatment	Posttest
O_A	C	1	X	O_2
O_A	C	2	—	O_2

Time ▶

Example for Diagram 3.2

Leake, M., & Lesik, S. A. (2007). Do remedial English programs impact first-year success in college? An illustration of the regression-discontinuity design. *International Journal of Research & Method in Education, 30*(1), 89–99.

Research Question: What are the effects of participating in a university remedial English program on first-year GPA?

Procedures: A total of 197 first-time university students' scores from an English placement examination were included in this study. An exogenous cutoff score was determined on the placement exam, and students who scored within a six-point range on either side of the cutoff score on the English placement examination were included in the analysis. Those who scored below the cutoff score, the treatment group ($n = 94$), were required to take a remedial English program. Those who scored above the cutoff score ($n = 103$) did not have to take any remedial courses. Upon completion of the remedial program assignment, the first-year GPA of both groups was included in the RD analysis.

Design: Quasi-experimental research utilizing a RD approach with a pretest-posttest control group design

Recommended parametric analysis: See Imbens and Lemieux (2008) for details.

Pretest	Assignment	Group	Treatment	Posttest
English placement examination	C	1 ($n = 94$)	Remedial English program	GPA
English placement examination	C	2 ($n = 103$)	—	GPA
Time ▶				

CHAPTER 4

WITHIN-SUBJECTS APPROACH

Major challenges when conducting research are often related to (a) access to participants and (b) an inability to randomly assign the participants to conditions. With these limitations in mind, researchers often employ a within-subjects approach. Although the pretest and posttest designs of between-subjects approaches include a within-subject component, the objective is not necessarily to test the within-subject variances as intended with within-subject approaches. The within-subjects approach to research assumes one group (or subject) serves in each of the treatment conditions. This approach is referred to as *repeated measures,* because participants are repeatedly measured across each condition. The advantage to this approach is that it can be utilized with smaller sample sizes with little or no error variance concerning individual differences between conditions (i.e., the same participants exist in each condition). Some disadvantages to this approach are maturation, history, and most importantly, the issue of sequencing effects (i.e., order and carryover effects). More specifically, performance in one treatment condition affects the performance in a second treatment condition. If possible, it is recommended to randomize the order of the treatments (also known as counterbalancing) to control for sequencing effects.

The simplest within-subjects approach is the one-group with a single pretest and posttest measure (quasi-experimental research one-factor design), which is presented here. This design can be extended to multiple pretest and posttest measures and is designated as an interrupted time-series

(ITS) design and sometimes called the "time-series" approach. For this guide, we categorize the ITS design under the repeated measures approach. Traditionally, it was believed that ITS designs should include upwards of 100 observations (in regard to statistical power), but many of these designs, when applied, often have anywhere from 10 to 50 observations and are often designated as short ITS designs.

REPEATED-MEASURES APPROACH ♦

Repeated-measures approaches are structured so the researcher can collect numerous measures from the participants. Specifically, designs that include repeated measures allow researchers to gather multiple data points over time to study the rate of change as a function of treatment or time. These types of designs typically are more advanced, which require advanced statistical analysis to summarize the data. Most single-case approaches must utilize repeated-measures approaches. This approach allows for the single unit of analysis to serve as its own control to minimize treatment effects. Designs that utilize repeated-measures approaches are also useful in longitudinal studies when examining trends or phenomena over a designated period of time. There are a variety of designs that utilize the repeated-measures approach. It is important to clarify that designs within the repeated-measures approach are classified as *experimental* so long as participants are randomly exposed to each condition (i.e., counterbalancing must occur because sequencing effects is the biggest threat to internal validity within this approach). The application of this approach, as with all approaches, is considered along with theoretical tenets and logistical considerations.

Repeated-measures approaches can also include a between-subjects component as seen in the pretest and multiple-posttest design and the switching replications design (the emphasis is usually on the between- and within-subject variances and sometimes are not referred to as repeated measures because technically each group is not exposed to each condition). We present one example of the pretest and multiple-posttest design and two examples of a switching-replication design (one experimental and one quasi-experimental). This design allows the researcher to assess the effects of the treatment on the first group while withholding the treatment to the second group. The second group is designated as a wait-list control group. This design includes only one treatment or factor. We also present a similar design, the crossover design (also known as a changeover design), which includes at a minimum two factors, but it can include more (Ryan, 2007; Shadish et al., 2002). Some researchers, as seen in the experimental example presented later, refer to a switching-replications design as a crossover design. To be clear, the switching-replications design includes one treatment and a wait-list control group, while the crossover design includes a minimum of two treatments and no control.

Crossover designs are the repeated-measures version of the k-factor design and are used to assess the order of effects of two or more factors (also known as multiple-treatment counterbalanced designs). When applying crossover designs it is important to ensure a "washout period," or return to baseline, between the adjacent treatment periods as a means to control for sequencing effects (i.e., multiple-treatment interference). These types of designs are ideal for eliminating issues associated with the between-subject variations and when a limited number of test subjects are available. However, if there are enough subjects to assign to groups to each condition, as seen in the 2-factor example presented later, then a between- and within-subject analysis should be used. Alternatively, a 3-factor model ($k = 3$; see Diagram 4.1), with one participant assigned to each condition, would require only a within-subjects analysis. The reader is referred to Hedayat, Stufken, and Yang (2006) for more examples of crossover designs.

Diagram 4.1 A Repeated-Measures Approach 3-Factor Crossover Design

Subject	Treatment	Midtest	Treatment	Midtest	Treatment	Posttest
1	X_A	O_1	X_B	O_2	X_C	O_3
2	X_B	O_1	X_C	O_2	X_A	O_3
3	X_C	O_1	X_A	O_2	X_B	O_3
4	X_C	O_1	X_B	O_2	X_A	O_3
5	X_A	O_1	X_C	O_2	X_B	O_3
6	X_B	O_1	X_A	O_2	X_C	O_3

Time ▶

Note: Each participant ($N = 6$) serves in one condition and the conditions are counterbalanced to control for sequencing effects. This design can be modified in multiple ways such as adding additional factors, introducing the same factor more than once in each condition, and including more observations.

We also present two examples of ITS designs. The basic ITS design includes one treatment (or factor) and many consecutive observations on the same outcome variable prior to and after the treatment. The number of pretest and posttest observations is based on theoretical, logistical, and statistical considerations. The first example includes two groups and one factor, and the second example includes one group and one factor. The strength of the ITS design is that it can account for the immediate and/or delayed effects of a treatment. The largest threats to internal validity for ITS designs are history and attrition. See Glass, Wilson, and Gottman (2008) for in-depth coverage of ITS designs and analysis.

Last, similar to the crossover design, we present an example of an $n \times n$ Latin-square design. The Latin-square design is a one-factor model with two nuisance or procedural factors (one for the rows and one for the columns), and it is most commonly applied in engineering, agriculture, and industrial research but rarely in the social sciences. However, there are instances within educational and the social and behavioral sciences in which a Latin-square design may be utilized. Within the Latin-square structure, each row and each column contain the treatment as a means to counterbalance the order of effects. A basic 3×3 Latin-square design can be applied, for example, if a researcher wishes to examine the effectiveness of three types of emotive imagery techniques (strong, medium, weak) on professional athletes' level of concentration (assuming a total of 75 athletes divided between each condition is adequate with regard to power). As seen in Diagram 4.2, the researcher would utilize three different settings (office, home, field) and three types of formats (live, recorded, combination) to administer the technique. This one-factor design includes emotive imagery (at three levels) and then two procedural factors (format and setting), each at three levels, hence the 3×3 framework.

Diagram 4.2 Example of a 3 × 3 Latin-Square Design

		Format		
Group	*Setting*	*Live*	*Recorded*	*Combo*
1 (*n* = 25)	Office	A	B	C
2 (*n* = 25)	Home	B	C	A
3 (*n* = 25)	Field	C	A	B

Note: A = Strong Emotive Imagery; B = Medium Emotive Imagery; C = Weak Emotive Imagery. Concentration would be assessed within each session. A general linear model one-way ANOVA is the appropriate analysis for this design.

This design is best applied in highly controlled conditions, and it is typically used as a means to protect against the effects of multiple extraneous variables. Some researchers utilize some form of a crossover design in their research and set up the rows and columns in the form of a Latin square.

However, it should be noted that without the inclusion of two procedural (blocking) factors, the examination does not take full advantage of the design characteristics for which the Latin-square design was originally created. The major assumption of this design is that there is no interaction (or very minimal) between rows and columns. The problem associated with this design when applied to the social sciences is the small number of observations for each combination of factor levels; in addition, when including humans as test subjects, the carryover effects are usually problematic (i.e., the efficiency of this design is application and data dependent). We refer the reader to McNemar (2007) for a discussion regarding the issues associated with the use of Latin-square designs in the social sciences. Based on the example scenario presented earlier, not every combination of imagery-format-setting is conducted. Theoretically, a $3 \times 3 \times 3$ factorial design may be a more suitable design for this application. Nonetheless, if the researcher wishes to include a third procedural factor (type of athlete, for example), then a Graeco-Latin–square design should be used (see Box, Hunter, and Hunter, 2005, p. 161, for more on Graeco-Latin-square designs). We also refer the reader to Reese (1997) for more information regarding the applications and analyses of Latin-square designs. We later present an example of a 6×6 Latin-square design.

Most common threats to internal validity are related, but not limited, to these designs:

> *Experimental:* History, Maturation, Testing, Instrumentation, Attrition, and Sequencing Effects

> *Quasi-Experimental:* History, Maturation, Testing, Instrumentation, Statistical Regression, Selection Bias, Attrition, and Sequencing Effects

The reader is referred to the following books for full explanations regarding research for repeated-measures approaches:

> Hinkelman, K., & Kempthorne, K. (2005). *Design and analysis of experiments, Volume 2: Advanced experimental designs.* Hoboken, NJ: Wiley.

> Spector, P. E. (1981). *Research designs.* Beverly Hills, CA: Sage.

Example for Diagram 4.3

Wyatt, T. H., & Hauenstein, E. J. (2008). Pilot test Okay With Asthma™: An online asthma intervention for school-age children. *The Journal of School Nursing, 24*(3), 145–150.

Research Question: What are the effects of the Okay With Asthma intervention on asthma knowledge and attitude in school-age children?

Diagram 4.3 Pretest and Posttest Design (One-Group)

Group	Pretest	Treatment	Posttest
1	O_1	X	O_2

Time ▶

Procedures: Thirty-five school-age children were recruited to participate in the study. During the first session, children completed the pretests and Okay With Asthma program under the supervision of the investigator. The investigator conducted a debriefing with each child after viewing the multimedia program. Following the end of the program, the children completed a round of posttest measures. The pretest and posttest measures included the Asthma Information quiz and the Child Attitude Toward Illness Scale.

Design: Quasi-experimental research utilizing a within-subjects approach and a one-group pretest and posttest design

Recommended parametric analysis: Descriptive statistics; dependent-samples t test or paired-samples t test (appropriate effect-size calculations should be included).

Assignment	Group	Pretest	Treatment	Posttest
NR	1 ($n = 35$)	Asthma Information quiz, Child Attitude Toward Illness Scale	Okay With Asthma™	Asthma Information quiz, Child Attitude Toward Illness Scale
			Time ▶	

Diagram 4.4 Pretest and Multiple-Posttest Design

Group	Pretest	Treatment	Posttest$_1$	Posttest$_2$
1	O_1	X	O_2	O_3
2	O_1	—	O_2	O_3

Time ▶

Note: Any number of posttests and factors can be included based on theoretical and logistical considerations.

Example for Diagram 4.4

Acee, T. W., & Weinstein, C. E. (2010). Effects of value-reappraisal intervention on statistics students' motivation and performance. *Journal of Experimental Education, 78*(4), 487–512.

Research Question: What are the effects of a value-reappraisal intervention on task value, endogenous instrumentality, self-efficacy, and exam performance?

Procedures: Participants were stratified based on instructor type, gender, and year in school, and then randomly assigned to each condition: the value-reappraisal (VR) group ($n = 41$) and the control group ($n = 41$). Both groups were assessed prior to the intervention on Task Value (TV), Endogenous Instrumentality (EI), self-efficacy (SE), and exam performance (EP). For the next three weeks, the students in the treatment group were exposed to the VR intervention, which was designed to help them reappraise their values of the statistics course. Immediately following the intervention, both groups received the TV, EI, SE, and EP assessments. Following a two-week delay, another round of the assessments was given.

Design: Experimental research utilizing a repeated-measures approach with a pretest and double-posttest design

Recommended parametric analysis: One-way RM-ANCOVA or one-way RM-MANCOVA (appropriate descriptive statistics and effect-size calculations should be included).

Example for Diagram 4.5

Cernin, P. A., & Lichtenberg, P. A. (2009). Behavioral treatment for depressed mood: A pleasant events intervention for seniors residing in assisted living. *Clinical Gerontologist, 32,* 324–331.

Assignment	Group	Pretest	Treatment	Posttest	Posttest (2-Week Delay)
R_s	1 ($n = 41$)	TV, EI, SE, EP	Value-Reappraisal	TV, EI, SE, EP	TV, EI, SE, EP
R_s	2 ($n = 41$)	TV, EI, SE, EP	—	TV, EI, SE, EP	TV, EI, SE, EP
Time ▶					

| Diagram 4.5 | Switching-Replications Design (Experimental) | | | | |

Group	Pretest	Treatment	Midtest	Treatment	Posttest
1	O_1	X_A	O_2	—	O_3
2	O_1	—	O_2	X_A	O_3

Time ▶

Research Question: What are the effects of pleasant-events–focused treatment on factors of mood and depression in older, frail adults?

Procedures: Participants were randomly assigned to either the immediate treatment condition ($n = 8$) or wait-list treatment condition ($n = 7$). Both groups received the same events-focused treatment. Data were collected by the project coordinator for all participants at baseline, three months, and six months. Participants enrolled in the immediate treatment condition received the intervention after baseline data collection in the first three months of the study. Participants enrolled in the wait-list treatment condition received the intervention between three and six months. Treatment consisted of pleasant-event activities mutually agreed upon with residents and was delivered in 30-minute sessions with a target goal of three sessions per week.

Design: Experimental research utilizing a repeated-measures approach with a switching replications design

Recommended parametric analysis: One-way RM-ANCOVA or one-way RM-MANCOVA (appropriate descriptive statistics and effect-size calculations should be included).

Example for Diagram 4.6

Basadur, M., Graen, G. B., & Scandura, T. A. (1986). Training effects on attitudes toward divergent thinking among manufacturing engineers. *Journal of Applied Psychology, 71*(4), 612–617.

Research Question: What are the effects of a training process of problem solving based on divergent thinking on engineers' attitudes?

Procedures: Initially, two groups of manufacturing engineers were identified as participants for the study. Group 1 ($n = 65$) was assigned to the first treatment

Assignment	Group	Pretest (Baseline)	Treatment	Midtest (3 months)	Treatment	Posttest (6 months)
R	1 (n = 8)	Mood, depression	Pleasant-events–focused treatment	Mood, depression	—	Mood, depression
R	2 (wait-list; n = 7)	Mood, depression	—	Mood, depression	Pleasant-events–focused treatment	Mood, depression
				Time ▶		

Note: The authors refer to this design as a crossover design; however, to qualify as a crossover design, it would require a minimum of two factors or treatments. Therefore, this is a switching replications design (Ryan, 2007; Shadish et al., 2002).

Diagram 4.6 Switching-Replications Design (Quasi-Experimental)

Group	Pretest	Treatment	Midtest	Treatment	Posttest
1	O_1	X_A	O_2	—	O_3
2	O_1	—	O_2	X_A	O_3
			Time ▶		

condition (creative problem-solving program) and group 2 ($n = 47$) was assigned to the wait-list control condition. Both groups were administered scales that measured the preferences for ideation in problem solving and a second scale that measured the premature convergence in problem solving. After five weeks, the measures were administered to both groups, and then the wait-list control went through the creative problem-solving program. Following the next five weeks, participants were administered the final posttest measures.

Design: Quasi-experimental research utilizing a repeated-measures approach with a switching replications design

Recommended parametric analysis: One-way reliability-corrected RM-ANCOVA or one-way reliability-corrected RM-MANCOVA (appropriate descriptive statistics and effect-size calculations should be included).

Assignment	Group	Pretest	Treatment	Midtest	Treatment	Posttest
NR	1 (*n* = 65)	Preference for ideation, premature evaluations	Creative problem-solving program	Preference for ideation, premature evaluations	—	Preference for ideation, premature evaluations
NR	2 (wait-list; *n* = 47)	Preference for ideation, premature evaluations	—	Preference for ideation, premature evaluations	Creative problem-solving program	Preference for ideation, premature evaluations
			Time ▶			

Diagram 4.7 Crossover Design (2-Factor)

Group	Pretest	Treatment	Midtest	Treatment	Posttest
1	O_1	X_A	O_2	X_B	O_3
2	O_1	X_B	O_2	X_A	O_3

Time ▶

Example for Diagram 4.7

Burgess, G., Grogan, S., & Burwitz, L. (2006). Effects of a 6-week aerobic dance intervention on body image and physical self-perceptions in adolescent girls. *Body Image, 3,* 57–66.

Research Question: What are the effects of an aerobic and physical education program on perceptions of body image?

Procedures: A total of 50 school-age girls (M_{age} = 13.5) were randomly assigned to one of two conditions. The first condition was an aerobic dance program and the second condition was physical education. Each condition lasted approximately six weeks. Following the completion of the first program, the participants changed over (crossover) to participate in the other treatment program. All participants were administered pretest, midtest, and posttest the Body Attitudes Questionnaire (BAQ), the Children and Youth Physical Self-Perceptions Profile (CY-PSPP), and the Leisure Time Physical Activity Questionnaire (LTPAQ).

Design: Experimental research utilizing a repeated-measures approach with a 2-factor crossover design

Assignment	Group	Pretest	Treatment	Midtest	Treatment	Posttest
R	1 (n = 25)	BAQ, CY-PSPP, LTPAQ	Aerobic dance	BAQ, CY-PSPP, LTPAQ	Physical education	BAQ, CY-PSPP, LTPAQ
R	2 (n = 25)	BAQ, CY-PSPP, LTPAQ	Physical education	BAQ, CY-PSPP, LTPAQ	Aerobic dance	BAQ, CY-PSPP, LTPAQ
			Time ▶			

Recommended parametric analysis: One-way RM-ANCOVA or one-way RM-MANCOVA (appropriate descriptive statistics and effect-size calculations should be included).

Diagram 4.8 Interrupted Time-Series Design (One-Group)

Group	Pretests	Treatment	Posttests
1	$O_1...O_8$	X	$O_7...O_{10}$
		Time ▶	

Note: Any number of pretest and posttest observations can be taken in an ITS design.

Example for Diagram 4.8

Rimondini, M., Del Piccolo, L., Goss, C., Mazzi, M., Paccaloni, M., & Zimmerman, C. (2010). The evaluation of training in patient-centered interviewing skills for psychiatric residents. *Psychological Medicine, 40,* 467–476.

Research Question: What is the impact of patient-centered interview training on patient-centered interviewing skills?

Procedures: A single group of psychiatric residents ($n = 10$) interviewed a total of 12 different patients. Each resident interviewed eight patients and was objectively tested by trained raters utilizing the Verona Psychiatric Interview Classification System (VR-PICS). The residents then went through a patient-centered skills training using the standards of the Verona Communication Skills Training in Psychiatry. The residents were then interviewed and were rated on a total of four more time points using the VR-PICS.

The major categories tested were gathering information, handling emotion, and handling doctor-centered issues, as well as an overall performance index.

Design: Quasi-experimental research utilizing a one-group interrupted time-series design

Recommended parametric analysis: Growth curve analysis, autoregressive integrated moving average (ARIMA), or time-series regression (appropriate descriptive statistics and effect-size calculations should be included).

Assignment	Group	Pretests 1–8	Treatment	Posttests 7–10
NR	1	VR-PICS	Verona Skills Training	VR-PICS
Time ▶				

Diagram 4.9 Interrupted Time-Series Design (Two-Group)

Group	Pretests	Treatment	Posttests
1	$O_1...O_6$		$O_7...O_{11}$
2	$O_1...O_6$	X	$O_7...O_{11}$

Time ▶

Example for Diagram 4.9

May, H., & Supovitz, J. A. (2006). Capturing the cumulative effects of school reform: An 11-year study of the impacts of America's Choice on student achievement. *Educational Evaluation and Policy Analysis, 28*(3), 231–257.

Research Question: What is the evidence of, and rate of increase in, learning in low-achieving and minority students in America's Choice programs?

Procedures: Eleven years of student performance school data were analyzed: 6 years of data before schools' adoption of the America's Choice program and up to 5 years after (depending on the year a school introduced the reform). During this period, more than 55,000 students in Grades 1 through 8, in

42 elementary and 10 middle schools, were tested in reading and mathematics. Multiple achievement tests during the 11-year span covered the study: (a) Stanford Achievement Test (SAT-9), (b) California Achievement Test (CAT-5), (c) Degrees of Reading Power test (DRP), (d) New York State assessments (NYS), (e) New York Pupil Evaluation Program tests (PEP), and (f) New York Preliminary Competency Test (PCT).

Design: Quasi-experimental research utilizing a two-group interrupted time-series design

Recommended parametric analysis: Growth curve analysis, autoregressive integrated moving average (ARIMA), or time-series regression (appropriate descriptive statistics and effect-size calculations should be included).

Assignment	Group	Years 1–6	Treatment	Years 7–11
NR	1 (Reading: n = 56,693)	SAT-9, CAT-5, DRP, NYS, PEP, PCT	America's Choice	SAT-9, CAT-5, DRP, NYS, PEP, PCT
NR	2 (Math: n = 55,932)	SAT-9, CAT-5, DRP, NYS, PEP, PCT		SAT-9, CAT-5, DRP, NYS, PEP, PCT
Time ▶				

Diagram 4.10 6 × 6 Latin-Square Design

Group	Conditions					
1	A	B	C	D	E	F
2	B	C	F	A	D	E
3	C	F	B	E	A	D
4	D	E	A	B	F	C
5	E	A	D	F	C	B
6	F	D	E	C	B	A
	Time ▶					

Note: There are many possible ordering variations of treatments in the Latin-square design, and the design presented here is only one example of a type of ordering.

Example for Diagram 4.10

Meijer, J., & Oostdam, R. (2007). Test anxiety and intelligence testing: A closer examination of the stage-fright hypothesis and the influence of stressful instruction. *Anxiety, Stress, and Coping, 20*(1), 77–91.

Research Question: What are the effects of text anxiety and style of instruction (stressful versus reassuring) on intelligence?

Procedures: A series of intelligence tests were administered to students over a 1-year time span. There were 135 students across six classes, and each class varied in size from 17 to 26 children. The age range was between 10 and 13 years old. The intelligence tests were taken from a version of the Netherlands Differentiation Test and included a vocabulary test, picture recall, dice and dominoes, verbal analogies, paired associates, and figure series. The administration of each test was counterbalanced for each class according to the Latin-square design. The first three tests for each class were administered under stressful conditions and the last three were administered under reassuring conditions. The Revised Worry-Emotionality Scale (RW-ES) was utilized to determine the level of perceived stress prior to each series of tests.

Design: Experimental research utilizing a 6 x 6 Latin-square design

Recommended parametric analysis: General linear models one-way ANOVA (appropriate descriptive statistics and effect-size calculations should be included).

Class (N = 135)	Stressful Instruction	Intelligence Tests			Reassuring Instruction	Intelligence Tests		
1	RW-ES	Voc	Pic	Dice	RW-ES	Ana	Pair	Fig
2	RW-ES	Pic	Dice	Ana	RW-ES	Pair	Fig	Voc
3	RW-ES	Dice	Ana	Pair	RW-ES	Fig	Voc	Pic
4	RW-ES	Ana	Pair	Fig	RW-ES	Voc	Pic	Dice
5	RW-ES	Pair	Fig	Voc	RW-ES	Pic	Dice	Ana
6	RW-ES	Fig	Voc	Pic	RW-ES	Dice	Ana	Pair
Time ▶								

Note: Voc = vocabulary; Pic = picture recall; Dice = dice and dominoes; Ana = verbal analogies; Pair = paired associates; Fig = figure series. This design is ordered as a Latin square; however, it does not follow the exact tenets of a Latin-square design (the lack of two blocking factors). Therefore, it can be considered a modified version of a repeated-measures 6-factor crossover design configured as a Latin square.

CHAPTER **5**

FACTORIAL DESIGNS

A n extension of the *k*-factor design is the factorial design. The simplest factorial design includes, at a minimum, two factors (i.e., independent variables), each with two levels (Kazdin, 2002; Vogt, 2005). Two factors each with two levels is designated as a 2 × 2 factorial design. Factorial designs are denoted by the form s^k. The *s* represents the number of levels and *k* represents the number of factors (e.g., 2 × 2 is the same as 2^2). Recall that a factor is another term for the independent variable, or treatment, or intervention.

Many *k*-factor designs can be transformed into factorial designs (based on theoretical and logistical considerations) by partitioning the factors into at least two levels and by subsequently changing the statistical analysis used to examine the data. For example, a researcher is interested in looking at the effects of a math intervention (factor) with two levels (1–visual math, 2–auditory math) and how it differs by gender (factor; 1–males, 2–females) on a math competency exam (i.e., dependent variable). Unlike the *k*-factor design, factorial designs allow for *all* combinations of the factor levels to be tested on the outcome (i.e., male and female differences for auditory style teaching compared to male and female differences for visual style teaching). Thus, factorial designs allow for the examination of both the *interaction* effects (the influence of one independent variable on the other independent variable) and the *main* effects (the influence of each independent variable on the outcome).

The factorial design is not one design; rather, it is considered a family of designs. For example, some research requires that the number of levels for each factor is not the same. The simplest version would be a 2 × 3 design (i.e., one independent variable has two levels and the other has three). Factorial designs can also include three factors (e.g., a 2 × 2 × 2 represents three independent variables, each with two levels). Factorial designs can be within subjects or can be between subjects, and they can include pretest and posttest or posttest-only measures (most contain only posttests). The within-subjects approach to factorial designs is set up so there is one group and each participant serves in each of the treatment conditions. The between-subjects approach allows the researcher to test multiple groups across conditions without exposing each participant to all treatment conditions. This approach requires larger sample sizes, and random assignment is highly recommended to control for differentiation and selection bias.

Another option to the factorial design is the mixed-subjects approach. A mixed-factorial design includes both a within- and between-subjects approach. For instance, a 2 × 3 mixed-factorial design would be constructed so the first factor at two levels is tested as within subjects, and the second factor at three levels would be tested as between subjects. To determine the number of groups (also referred to as cells), the number of levels for each factor can be multiplied (e.g., 2 × 2 = 4 groups; 2 × 3 = 6 groups). The strength of this design is that it allows a researcher to examine the individual and combined effects of the variables. There are many types and variations of factorial designs not illustrated in this reference guide.

We provide three examples of a 2-factor between-subjects factorial design (a pretest and posttest design [2 × 2], two posttest-only designs [2 × 2 and 3 × 2]) and one example of a 2 × 2 within-subjects factorial design). We also provide two examples of a between-subjects factorial design with three factors (2 × 2 × 2 and 2 × 3 × 2) and one example of a mixed-factorial design (2 × 2 × 2).

Factorial designs that include within-subjects components are also affected by the threats to internal validity listed under the repeated-measures approach (e.g., Sequencing Effects).

Most common threats to internal validity are related, but not limited, to these designs:

Experimental: Maturation, Testing, Diffusion, and Instrumentation

Quasi-Experimental: Maturation, Testing, Instrumentation, Diffusion, and Selection Bias

The reader is referred to the following book for full explanations regarding factorial designs:

Ryan, T. P. (2007). *Modern experimental design.* Hoboken, NJ: Wiley.

Diagram 5.1	2 × 2 Factorial Pretest and Posttest Design (Between-Subjects)

Group	Pretest	Treatment	Posttest
1	O_1	X_{A1B1}	O_2
2	O_1	X_{A1B2}	O_2
3	O_1	X_{A2B1}	O_2
4	O_1	X_{A2B2}	O_2

Time ▶

Example for Diagram 5.1

Stern, S. E., Mullennix, J. W., & Wilson, S. J. (2002). Effects of perceived disability on persuasiveness of computer-synthesized speech. *Journal of Applied Psychology, 87*(2), 411–417.

Research Question (main and interaction effects): What are the effects of perceived disabilities on the persuasiveness of computer-synthesized and normal speech?

Procedures: Participants completed an attitude pretest and were randomly assigned to watch an actor deliver a persuasive speech under one of the following four conditions: (a) disabled using normal speech, (b) nondisabled using normal speech, (c) disabled using computer-synthesized speech, or (d) nondisabled using computer-synthesized speech. Participants then completed an attitude posttest survey. Additionally, the following posttest measures not included in the factorial analysis were collected: (a) questionnaires assessing attitudes, (b) perceptions of voice characteristics, and (c) the effectiveness of the message.

Design: Experimental research utilizing a between-subjects approach 2 × 2 factorial pretest and posttest design.

Recommended parametric analysis: 2-way factorial ANCOVA or 2-way factorial MANCOVA (appropriate descriptive statistics and effect-size calculations should be included).

Assignment	Group	Pretest	Factor *Ability (A)*	Factor *Speech Type (B)*	Posttest
R	1	Attitudes	Disabled (A$_1$)	Synthetic speech (B$_1$)	Attitudes, speech characteristics, effectiveness of message
R	2	Attitudes	Disabled (A$_1$)	Normal speech (B$_2$)	Attitudes, speech characteristics, effectiveness of message
R	3	Attitudes	Nondisabled (A$_2$)	Synthetic speech (B$_1$)	Attitudes, speech characteristics, effectiveness of message
R	4	Attitudes	Nondisabled (A$_2$)	Normal speech (B$_2$)	Attitudes, speech characteristics, effectiveness of message
			Time ▶		

2 × 2 (N = 189)	Independent Variable *Ability (A)*	
Independent Variable *Speech Type (B)*	*Disabled (A$_1$)*	*Nondisabled (A$_2$)*
Computer-synthesized speech (B$_1$)	*n* = 48	*n* = 47
Natural speech (B$_2$)	*n* = 47	*n* = 47

Diagram 5.2   2 × 2 Factorial Posttest Design (Between-Subjects)

Group	Treatment	Posttest
1	X$_{A1B1}$	O$_1$
2	X$_{A1B2}$	O$_1$
3	X$_{A2B1}$	O$_1$
4	X$_{A2B2}$	O$_1$
	Time ▶	

Example for Diagram 5.2

Sidani, Y. M. (2007). Perceptions of leader transformational ability: The role of leader speech and follower self-esteem. *Journal of Management Development, 26*(8), 710–722.

Research Questions

- *Main effect:* Are individuals with low self-esteem more prone to the transformational relationship? Do leader speeches characterized by a good use of rhetorical devices lead to higher levels of attributed transformational abilities?
- *Interaction effect:* Does the interaction of the transformational leader style with inspirational speech lead to greater attributions of transformational leadership than when either or both of these components are absent? Does the interaction of the nontransformational leader style with noninspirational speech lead to lower attributions of transformational leadership compared to other interactions?

Procedures: Participants were students enrolled in undergraduate business courses in a North American university. The participants were randomly assigned to one of four groups: (a) inspirational speech by a transformational leader ($n = 81$), (b) noninspirational speech by a transformational leader ($n = 77$), (c) inspirational speech by a transactional leader ($n = 76$), and (d) noninspirational speech by a transactional leader ($n = 79$). Leadership style was manipulated by developing two leadership profiles describing the differences between transactional and transformational leaders. Next, participants were presented either with a noninspirational speech or an inspirational speech. All participants completed posttests on the Multifactor Leadership Questionnaire.

Design: Experimental research utilizing a between-subjects approach 2×2 factorial posttest design

Recommended parametric analysis: 2-way factorial ANOVA or 2-way factorial MANOVA (appropriate descriptive statistics and effect-size calculations should be included).

Example for Diagram 5.3

Lopez, E. N., Drobes, D. J., Thompson, K. J., & Brandon, T. H. (2008). Effects of body image challenge on smoking motivation among college females. *Health Psychology, 27*(3), 243–251.

Assignment	Group	Factor Leader Type (A)	Factor Speech Type (B)	Posttest
R	1	Transformational (A₁)	Inspirational speech (B₁)	Multifactor Leadership Questionnaire
R	2	Transformational (A₁)	Noninspirational speech (B₂)	Multifactor Leadership Questionnaire
R	3	Transactional (A₂)	Inspirational speech (B₁)	Multifactor Leadership Questionnaire
R	4	Transactional (A₂)	Noninspirational speech (B₂)	Multifactor Leadership Questionnaire
			Time ▶	

2×2 (N = 313)	Independent Variable Leader Type (A)	
Independent Variable Speech Type (B)	Transformational (A₁)	Transactional (A₂)
Inspirational (B₁)	$n = 81$	$n = 76$
Noninspirational (B₂)	$n = 77$	$n = 79$

Diagram 5.3 2×2 Factorial Pretest and Posttest Design (Within-Subjects)

Group	Pretest	Treatment	Posttest
1	O_1	X_{A1B1}	O_2
1	O_1	X_{A1B2}	O_2
1	O_1	X_{A2B1}	O_2
1	O_1	X_{A2B2}	O_2
		Time ▶	

Research Questions: Does state body dissatisfaction lead to a situational increase in smoking motivation among young college females? Do individuals with greater trait body dissatisfaction show the greatest impact of the body image challenge on smoking urges?

Procedures: Sixty-two participants were recruited to participate in the study. Participants were exposed to pairs of cues associated with each factor simultaneously on a split screen. Thus, the four conditions were thin models/smoking cues, thin models/neutral cues, neutral cues/smoking cues, and neutral cues/neutral cues. Initially, participants completed measures assessing basic demographics, Smoking Status Questionnaire (SSQ), and the Short-Smoking Consequences Questionnaire (Short-SCQ). The order of the treatment conditions were randomized for all the participants. The in-test and posttest measures included the Eating Disorders Examination-Questionnaire Version-Weight Concern subscale (EDEQ-WC), the Urge to Smoke Visual Analogue Scale (Smoke VAS), and the Weight Dissatisfaction Visual Analogue Scale (Weight Dissatisfaction VAS).

Design: Experimental research utilizing a within-subjects approach 2×2 factorial pretest and posttest design

Recommended parametric analysis: 2-way factorial ANCOVA or 2-way factorial MANCOVA (appropriate descriptive statistics and effect-size calculations should be included).

Group	Pretest	Factor *Body Image (A)*	Factor *Smoking Cue (B)*	In-Test/Posttest
1	SSQ, Short-SCQ	Thin (A_1)	Smoking (B_1)	EDEQ-WC, Smoke VAS, Weight Dissatisfaction VAS
1	SSQ, Short-SCQ	Thin (A_1)	Neutral (B_2)	EDEQ-WC, Smoke VAS, Weight Dissatisfaction VAS
1	SSQ, Short-SCQ	Neutral (A_2)	Smoking (B_1)	EDEQ-WC, Smoke VAS, Weight Dissatisfaction VAS
1	SSQ, Short-SCQ	Neutral (A_2)	Neutral (B_2)	EDEQ-WC, Smoke VAS, Weight Dissatisfaction VAS
Time ▶				

Note: The authors refer to the design as a randomized factorial design, which means the order of the treatments was randomized (i.e., counterbalanced) for each participant to control for sequencing effects.

2 × 2 (N = 62)	**Independent Variable** *Body Image Manipulation (A)*	
Independent Variable *Smoking Cue (B)*	Thin (A₁)	Neutral (A₂)
Smoking (B₁)	$n = 62$	$n = 62$
Neutral (B₂)	$n = 62$	$n = 62$

Note: Each cell represents the same participants (i.e., within-subjects).

Diagram 5.4   3 × 2 Factorial Posttest Design (Between-Subjects)

Group	Treatment	Posttest
1	X_{A1B1}	O_1
2	X_{A2B1}	O_1
3	X_{A3B1}	O_1
4	X_{A1B2}	O_1
5	X_{A2B2}	O_1
6	X_{A3B2}	O_1

Time ▶

Example for Diagram 5.4

Gier, V. S., Kreiner, D. S., & Natz-Gonzalez, A. (2009). Harmful effects of preexisting inappropriate highlighting on reading comprehension and metacognitive accuracy. *The Journal of General Psychology, 136*(3), 287–300.

Research Questions

- *Main effect:* Does inappropriate highlighting reduce performance on a comprehension test in comparison with no highlighting and appropriate highlighting? Does inappropriate highlighting result in reduced ability to monitor comprehension and test performance? Does more difficult reading material result in lower comprehension and metacognitive accuracy?
- *Interaction effect:* Do metacognitive accuracy and comprehension scores differ with respect to text difficulty as a result of no highlighting, appropriate highlighting, and inappropriate highlighting?

Procedures: Participants were 180 undergraduate students from a southeastern university in the United States. The researchers manipulated text difficulty (two levels) and type of highlighting (three levels). Participants read texts that were either (a) not highlighted (control group), (b) appropriately highlighted (i.e., the sentences relevant to the comprehension questions were highlighted), or (c) inappropriately highlighted (i.e., the sentences highlighted were not relevant to the comprehension questions). Participants were randomly assigned to one of the six conditions. Immediately after reading each passage, participants provided metacomprehension ratings by recording how well they thought they had comprehended the passage. Then, participants responded to the comprehension test, which consisted of six multiple-choice questions. After responding to the comprehension questions, participants provided confidence ratings that their answers were correct. The researchers measured and scored all of the metacomprehension visual analogue and comprehension scales.

Design: Experimental research utilizing a between-subjects approach 3 × 2 factorial posttest design

Recommended parametric analysis: 2-way factorial ANOVA or 2-way factorial MANOVA (appropriate descriptive statistics and effect-size calculations should be included).

Example for Diagram 5.5

Baylor, A. L., & Kim, S. (2009). Designing nonverbal communication for pedagogical agents: When less is more. *Computers in Human Behavior, 25,* 450–457.

Research Questions

- *Main effect:* What is the effect of types of instruction, deictic gestures, and types of facial expressions on student perceptions of pedagogical agent persona, attitude toward content, and learning?
- *Interaction effect:* Is there an interaction effect between the type of instruction and agent nonverbal behavior?

Procedures: A total of 236 undergraduate students participated in this study. The participants were randomly assigned to one of eight treatment conditions (roughly $n = 29$ per cell). The three major factors (independent variables)

Assignment	Group	Factor *Highlighted (A)*	Factor *Text Difficulty (B)*	Posttest
R	1	None (A$_1$)	Low (B$_1$)	Metacomprehension scale, comprehension test, confidence
R	2	Appropriate (A$_2$)	Low (B$_1$)	Metacomprehension scale, comprehension test, confidence
R	3	Inappropriate (A$_3$)	Low (B$_1$)	Metacomprehension scale, comprehension test, confidence
R	4	None (A$_1$)	High (B$_2$)	Metacomprehension scale, comprehension test, confidence
R	5	Appropriate (A$_2$)	High (B$_2$)	Metacomprehension scale, comprehension test, confidence
R	6	Inappropriate (A$_3$)	High (B$_2$)	Metacomprehension scale, comprehension test, confidence

Time ▶

2 × 3 (N = 180)	Independent Variable *Highlighted Reading Passages (A)*		
Independent Variable *Text Difficulty (B)*	None (A$_1$)	Appropriate (A$_2$)	Inappropriate (A$_3$)
Low (B$_1$)	n = 30	n = 30	n = 30
High (B$_2$)	n = 30	n = 30	n = 30

Diagram 5.5 2 × 2 × 2 Factorial Posttest Design (Between-Subjects)

Group	Treatment	Posttest		Group	Treatment	Posttest
1	X$_{A1B1C1}$	O$_1$		5	X$_{A1B1C2}$	O$_1$
2	X$_{A1B2C1}$	O$_1$		6	X$_{A1B2C2}$	O$_1$
3	X$_{A2B1C1}$	O$_1$		7	X$_{A2B1C2}$	O$_1$
4	X$_{A2B2C1}$	O$_1$		8	X$_{A2B2C2}$	O$_1$

Time ▶ Time ▶

Note: For ease of reading, groups 1–4 and 5–8 have been placed side by side, but (for example) groups 1 and 5 are not related.

were each portioned into two levels: type of instruction (procedural, attitudinal), deictic gestures (presence, absence), and facial expressions (presence, absence). The two major modules developed were the procedural and attitudinal. The participants were exposed to the conditions during a computer literacy course. Following the exposure to the modules and conditions, the participants were assessed in three different areas: perceptions of agent persona, attitudes, and learning. The perceptions were assessed with the Agent Persona Instrument (API).

Design: Experimental research utilizing a between-subjects approach 2 × 2 × 2 factorial posttest design

Recommended parametric analysis: 3-way factorial ANOVA or 3-way factorial MANOVA (appropriate descriptive statistics and effect-size calculations should be included).

Assignment	Group	Factor Instruction Type (A)	Factor Deictic Gesture (B)	Factor Facial Expression (C)	Posttest
R	1	Procedural (A_1)	Presence (B_1)	Presence (C_1)	API, attitudes, learning
R	2	Procedural (A_1)	Absence (B_2)	Presence (C_1)	API, attitudes, learning
R	3	Attitudinal (A_2)	Presence (B_1)	Presence (C_1)	API, attitudes, learning
R	4	Attitudinal (A_2)	Absence (B_2)	Presence (C_1)	API, attitudes, learning
R	5	Procedural (A_1)	Presence (B_1)	Absence (C_2)	API, attitudes, learning
R	6	Procedural (A_1)	Absence (B_2)	Absence (C_2)	API, attitudes, learning
R	7	Attitudinal (A_2)	Presence (B_1)	Absence (C_2)	API, attitudes, learning
R	8	Attitudinal (A_2)	Absence (B_2)	Absence (C_2)	API, attitudes, learning
Time ▶					

2 × 2 × 2	**Independent Variable (IV)** *Instruction Type (A)*		N = 236
IV Deictic Gesture (B)	Procedural Module (A$_1$)	Attitudinal Module (A$_2$)	**IV** Facial Expression (C)
Presence (B$_1$)	n = 29	n = 30	Presence C$_1$
Absence (B$_2$)	n = 29	n = 30	Absence C$_1$
Presence (B$_1$)	n = 29	n = 30	Presence C$_2$
Absence (B$_2$)	n = 29	n = 30	Absence C$_2$

Diagram 5.6 2 × 3 × 2 Factorial Posttest Design (Between-Subjects)

Group	Treatment	Posttest		Group	Treatment	Posttest
1	X$_{A1B1C1}$	O$_1$		7	X$_{A1B1C2}$	O$_1$
2	X$_{A1B2C1}$	O$_1$		8	X$_{A1B2C2}$	O$_1$
3	X$_{A1B3C1}$	O$_1$		9	X$_{A1B3C2}$	O$_1$
4	X$_{A2B1C1}$	O$_1$		10	X$_{A2B1C2}$	O$_1$
5	X$_{A2B2C1}$	O$_1$		11	X$_{A2B2C2}$	O$_1$
6	X$_{A2B3C1}$	O$_1$		12	X$_{A2B3C2}$	O$_1$
	Time ▶				Time ▶	

Note: For ease of reading, groups 1–6 and 7–12 were placed side by side, but (for example) groups 1 and group 7 are not related.

Example for Diagram 5.6

Young, P., & Miller-Smith, K. (2006). Effects of state mandated policy (site-based councils) and of potential role incumbents on teacher screening decisions in high and low performing schools. *Education Policy and Analysis Archives, 14*(7), 1–21.

Research Questions

- *Main effect:* What are the effects of state-mandated policy and the potential role of incumbents on teacher screening in high and low performing schools?
- *Interaction effect:* Does legislative action, the role of the evaluator, and accountability differ with respect to perceived skill levels and the willingness to select a candidate?

Procedures: Public school administrators from two neighboring states participated in this study. A total of 624 participants were randomly selected from these locations. Three factors (independent variables) were evaluated in this study. The first was the state-legislative process, which was broken down into two levels: site-based and non-site-based. The next factor was the role of the evaluator within the teacher-screening process. The screening process (i.e., role of the evaluator) was portioned into principals, teachers, and parents. The third factor was the academic performance of public school districts and was broken down into high and low performers. All the participants were randomly assigned to 1 of 12 conditions. Each participant was assessed on two dependent variables. The first outcome variable measured the candidate's perceived skill level in relation to the job-related criteria. The second outcome variable measured the willingness that an evaluator (teacher, principal, or parent) would consider a candidate for an interview.

Design: Experimental research utilizing a between-subjects approach $2 \times 3 \times 2$ factorial posttest design

Recommended parametric analysis: Three-way factorial ANOVA or three-way factorial MANOVA (appropriate descriptive statistics and effect-size calculations should be included).

Example for Diagram 5.7

Guadagno, R. E., & Sagarin, B. J. (2010). Sex differences in jealousy: An evolutionary perspective on online infidelity. *Journal of Applied Social Psychology, 40*(10), 2636–2655.

Research Questions

- *Main effect:* What is the effect of infidelity context and type on perceptions of jealousy? Are there differences in regard to gender?
- *Interaction effect:* Is there an interaction effect between infidelity and context?

Procedures: A total of 332 undergraduate students ($n = 132$ males; $n = 200$ females) participated in this study. The participants were randomly assigned to one of eight treatment conditions (between 30 and 50 per cell). The three major factors (independent variables) were each portioned into two levels: infidelity context (online or conventional), gender (male or female), and infidelity type (sexual or emotional). Infidelity context and gender were

Assignment	Group	Factor Legislative Action (A)	Factor Role of Evaluator (B)	Factor Accountability (C)	Posttest
R	1	Site-based (A₁)	Principal (B₁)	Low (C₁)	Perceived skill level, willingness to select candidate
R	2	Site-based (A₁)	Teacher (B₂)	Low (C₁)	Perceived skill level, willingness to select candidate
R	3	Site-based (A₁)	Parent (B₃)	Low (C₁)	Perceived skill level, willingness to select candidate
R	4	Non-site-based (A₂)	Principal (B₁)	Low (C₁)	Perceived skill level, willingness to select candidate
R	5	Non-site-based (A₂)	Teacher (B₂)	Low (C₁)	Perceived skill level, willingness to select candidate
R	6	Non-site-based (A₂)	Parent (B₃)	Low (C₁)	Perceived skill level, willingness to select candidate
R	7	Site-based (A₁)	Principal (B₁)	High (C₂)	Perceived skill level, willingness to select candidate
R	8	Site-based (A₁)	Teacher (B₂)	High (C₂)	Perceived skill level, willingness to select candidate
R	9	Site-based (A₁)	Parent (B₃)	High (C₂)	Perceived skill level, willingness to select candidate
R	10	Non-site-based (A₂)	Principal (B₁)	High (C₂)	Perceived skill level, willingness to select candidate
R	11	Non-site-based (A₂)	Teacher (B₂)	High (C₂)	Perceived skill level, willingness to select candidate
R	12	Non-site-based (A₂)	Parent (B₃)	High (C₂)	Perceived skill level, willingness to select candidate

Time ▶

$2 \times 3 \times 2$	IV Role of Evaluator (B)			N = 624
IV Legislative Action (A)	Principal (B₁)	Teacher (B₂)	Parent (B₃)	IV Accountability (C)
Site-based (A₁)	n = 52	n = 52	n = 52	Low (C₁)
Non-site-based (A₂)	n = 52	n = 52	n = 52	Low (C₁)
Site-based (A₁)	n = 52	n = 52	n = 52	High (C₂)
Non-site-based (A₂)	n = 52	n = 52	n = 52	High (C₂)

Diagram 5.7 2 × 2 × 2 Mixed-Factorial Design (Mixed-Subjects)

Group	Treatment	Posttest
1	$X_{A1B1\ C1C2}$	O_1
2	$X_{A1B2\ C1C2}$	O_1
3	$X_{A2B1\ C1C2}$	O_1
4	$X_{A2B2\ C1C2}$	O_1

Time ▶

Group	Treatment	Posttest
5	$X_{A1B1\ C2C1}$	O_1
6	$X_{A1B2\ C2C1}$	O_1
7	$X_{A2B1\ C2C1}$	O_1
8	$X_{A2B2\ C2C1}$	O_1

Time ▶

Note: In this particular study, the third factor (Independent Variable: C1 and C2) was the variable treated as the within-subjects condition. Therefore, all eight groups were exposed to both levels of factor C (1 and 2).

between subjects, and infidelity type is within subjects. The participants were then exposed to one of two hypothetical scenarios, which included a series of questions related to emotional and sexual infidelity either in an online environment or in a conventional environment. Following the exposure, the participants were asked to complete a survey to assess their level of jealousy.

Design: Experimental research utilizing a 2 × 2 × 2 mixed-factorial design.

Recommended parametric analysis: 3-way factorial ANOVA or 3-way factorial MANOVA (appropriate descriptive statistics and effect-size calculations should be included).

Assign	Group	Factor (BS) Infidelity Context (A)	Factor (BS) Gender (B)	Factor (WS) Infidelity Type (C)	Posttest
R	1	Online (A$_1$)	Male (B$_1$)	Emotional (C$_1$) and Sexual (C$_2$)	Test
R	2	Online (A$_1$)	Female (B$_2$)	Emotional (C$_1$) and Sexual (C$_2$)	Test
R	3	Conventional (A$_2$)	Male (B$_1$)	Emotional (C$_1$) and Sexual (C$_2$)	Test
R	4	Conventional (A$_2$)	Female (B$_2$)	Emotional (C$_1$) and Sexual (C$_2$)	Test
R	5	Online (A$_1$)	Male (B$_1$)	Sexual (C$_2$) and Emotional (C$_1$)	Test
R	6	Online (A$_1$)	Female (B$_2$)	Sexual (C$_2$) and Emotional (C$_1$)	Test
R	7	Conventional (A$_2$)	Male (B$_1$)	Sexual (C$_2$) and Emotional (C$_1$)	Test
R	8	Conventional (A$_2$)	Female (B$_2$)	Sexual (C$_2$) and Emotional (C$_1$)	Test
			Time ▶		

Note: Factors A and B were treated as between subjects and factor C was treated as within subjects (BS = between subjects; WS = within subjects).

2 × 2 × 2	Independent Variable (IV) Infidelity Context (A)		N = 332
IV Gender (B)	Online (A$_1$)	Conventional (A$_2$)	IV Infidelity Type (C)
Male (B$_1$)	n = 33	n = 33	Emotional (C$_1$) and Sexual (C$_2$)
Female (B$_2$)	n = 50	n = 50	Emotional (C$_1$) and Sexual (C$_2$)
Male (B$_1$)	n = 33	n = 33	Emotional (C$_1$) and Sexual (C$_2$)
Female (B$_2$)	n = 50	n = 50	Emotional (C$_1$) and Sexual (C$_2$)

CHAPTER 6

SOLOMON
N-GROUP DESIGN

T he Solomon four-group design (Solomon, 1949) was developed specifically to combine the strengths of both types of between-subjects approaches (pretest only and the pretest and posttest design) as a means to minimize the weaknesses associated with using only one type. As a result, most of the major threats to internal validity (e.g., testing) and construct validity (e.g., pretest sensitization) are minimized. The inclusion of a control (or comparison) group to a research design can strengthen the internal validity and the overall validity of the findings. However, as noted earlier, there are strengths and costs in using between-subjects pretest and posttest control group designs compared to that of between-subjects posttest-only control group designs. The Solomon four-group design is an extension of the factorial design and is considered one of the strongest experimental designs, but its application in the social sciences is uncommon. Many investigators believe that logistical considerations (e.g., time, costs, number of participants, statistical analysis) are too much to overcome when applying this design. Although Solomon's original work did not include a sound statistical analysis for this design, researchers have attempted to offer statistical solutions and recommendations for power analysis (Sawilowsky, Kelley, Blair, & Markman, 1994; Walton Braver & Braver, 1988).

Originally, the Solomon four-group design was developed to include only four groups. Specifically, the four-group design includes one treatment (or factor; $k = 1$), with group 1 receiving the treatment with a pretest and posttest, group 2 receiving the pretest and posttest with no treatment, group 3 receiving the treatment and only a posttest, and finally group 4 receiving only the post-test. This allows the researcher to assess the main effects, as well as interaction effects between the pretest and no-pretest conditions. However, it has been proposed that the original design can include more than one treatment, thus extending the design to six groups for two-factor models or eight groups for three-factor models (i.e., Solomon *N*-group design). These designs allow researchers to test the effects of more than one type of treatment intervention against one another. Therefore, the design can be referred to as a Solomon four-, six-, or eight-group design. We present examples of research that utilized a Solomon four-group design ($k = 1$), one example of a six-group design ($k = 2$), and one example of an eight-group design ($k = 3$).

Most common threats to internal validity are related, but not limited, to these designs:

> *Experimental:* This design controls for all threats to internal validity except for Instrumentation.

> *Quasi-Experimental:* Instrumentation and Selection Bias

The reader is referred to the following article for full explanations and recommended analyses regarding Solomon four-, six-, and eight-group designs:

> Steyn, R. (2009). Re-designing the Solomon four-group: Can we improve on this exemplary model? *Design Principles and Practices: An International Journal, 3*(1), 1833–1874.

Diagram 6.1 Solomon Four-Group Design

Group	Pretest	Treatment	Posttest
1	O_1	X_A	O_2
2	O_3	—	O_4
3	—	X_A	O_5
4	—	—	O_6

Time ▶

Note: It is highly recommended that random assignment be used when applying the Solomon *N*-group designs.

Example for Diagram 6.1

Probst, T. M. (2003). Exploring employee outcomes of organizational restructuring. *Group & Organization Management, 28*(3), 416–439.

Research Questions

- *Main effect:* Does job security, job satisfaction, commitment, physical and mental health decline, and turnover intention increase following the announcement and implementation of organizational restructuring? Do individuals who are affected by organizational restructuring report lower levels of job security, less job satisfaction, more negative affective reactions, greater intentions to quit, lower levels of physical and mental health, higher levels of role ambiguity, and higher levels of time pressure than individuals not affected by organizational restructuring?
- *Interaction effect:* The authors of this study did not explore interaction effects. A 2 × 2 factorial design would allow for the examination of the interactions within a Solomon four-group design. In this study, each independent variable has two levels (treatment and no-treatment; pretest and no-pretest). See the chart that follows for an example of a 2 × 2 factorial design for this study.

Procedures: A stratified random sample of 500 employees from five state agencies going through reorganization was selected. The stratification was based on whether the employee was affected by the reorganization. A total of 313 employees (63% of the sample) participated in the study. The sample was divided into two groups, those affected by the reorganization ($n = 147$) and those unaffected by the reorganization ($n = 166$). In addition, all participants were randomly assigned to either a pretest ($n = 126$) or no pretest ($n = 187$) group. Data were collected at two different time points: (a) immediately prior to the workplace reorganization announcement and (b) 6 months following the merger announcement. There were four different groups of participants: (a) pretested and affected by the reorganization, (b) pretested but unaffected by the reorganization, (c) affected but not pretested, and (d) unaffected and pretested. A survey assessing each of the variables (see Research Questions) of interest was administered prior to the merger announcement and 6 months into the reorganization.

Design: Experimental research utilizing a between-subjects approach and a Solomon four-group design

Recommended parametric analysis: 2-way factorial ANOVA or maximum likelihood regression (appropriate descriptive statistics and effect-size calculations should be included).

Assignment	Group	Pretest	Treatment	Posttest
R	1 (n = 64)	Survey	Organizational restructuring	Survey
R	2 (n = 62)	Survey	—	Survey
R	3 (n = 83)	—	Organizational restructuring	Survey
R	4 (n = 104)	—	—	Survey
			Time ▶	

2 × 2 (n = 313)	**Independent Variable** Organizational Restructure (X)	
Independent Variable Pretest	Yes	No
Yes	n = 64 (O_2)	n = 62 (O_4)
No	n = 83 (O_5)	n = 104 (O_6)

Note: O_2, for example, represents the posttest observation for group 1 from the design structure.

Diagram 6.2 Solomon Six-Group Design

Group	Pretest	Treatment	Posttest
1	O_1	X_A	O_2
2	O_3	X_B	O_4
3	—	X_A	O_5
4	—	X_B	O_6
5	O_7	—	O_8
6	—	—	O_9
	Time ▶		

Note: The study had two treatment conditions (fake-good [X_A] and fake-bad [X_B]) with one control and one pretest-posttest no treatment group serving both treatment conditions; thus, technically, it is a Solomon six-group design, although the authors refer to it as a four-group design.

Example for Diagram 6.2

Whitman, D. S., Van Rooy, D. L., Viswesvaran, C., & Alonso, A. (2008). The susceptibility of a mixed model measure of emotional intelligence to faking: A Solomon four-group design. *Psychology Science, 50*(1), 44–63.

Research Questions

- *Main effect:* Do individual differences influence the extent to which emotional intelligence (EI) can be faked? To what extent do individual differences affect how much EI can be faked? Does a within-subjects design produce a higher effect size than a between subjects design?
- *Interaction effect:* Was there an interaction effect between pretesting and faking instructions?

Procedures: The study included a sample of 300 undergraduate psychology students. Three measures were collected from different groups at different time points during the course of the study: (a) general mental ability (GMA), (b) personality (IPI), and (c) emotional intelligence (EIS). All participants were randomly assigned to one of six experimental conditions and each group took the EIS, either (a) once under respond honest instructions and then once under fake-good instructions (group 1); (b) once under respond honest instructions and then once under fake-bad instructions (group 2); (c) only once (no pretest) under fake-good instructions (group 3); (d) only once (no pretest) under fake-bad instructions (group 4); (e) twice, both times under "respond honest" instructions (group 5); or (f) one time (no pretest) under "respond honest" instructions (group 6). Only one control group (group 6) and only one no treatment pretest-posttest group (group 5) were used for both the fake-good and fake-bad conditions.

Design: Experimental research utilizing a within and between-subjects approach and a Solomon six-group design

Recommended parametric analysis: 2-way factorial ANOVA, hierarchical multiple regression, or maximum likelihood regression (appropriate descriptive statistics and effect-size calculations should be included).

Assignment	Group	Pretest	Treatment	Posttest
R	1 ($n = 50$)	GMA, IPI, EIS	Fake-Good	GMA, IPI, EIS
R	2 ($n = 50$)	GMA, IPI, EIS	Fake-Bad	GMA, IPI, EIS
R	3 ($n = 50$)	—	Fake-Good	GMA, IPI, EIS
R	4 ($n = 50$)	—	Fake-Bad	GMA, IPI, EIS
R	5 ($n = 50$)	GMA, IPI, EIS	—	GMA, IPI, EIS
R	6 ($n = 50$)	—	—	GMA, IPI, EIS
Time ▶				

Note: Groups 5 and 6 did not receive the treatment (i.e., were not told to fake-good or fake-bad) and completed the EIS with the instruction to respond honestly.

2 × 2 (n = 200)	**Independent Variable** Fake-Good (X_A)	
Independent Variable Pretest	Yes	No
Yes	$n = 50$ (O_2)	$n = 50$ (O_8)
No	$n = 50$ (O_5)	$n = 50$ (O_9)

2 × 2 (n = 200)	**Independent Variable** Fake-Bad (X_B)	
Independent Variable Pretest	Yes	No
Yes	$n = 50$ (O_4)	$n = 50$ (O_8)
No	$n = 50$ (O_6)	$n = 50$ (O_9)

| Diagram 6.3 | Solomon Eight-Group Design |

Group	Pretest	Treatment	Posttest
1	O_1	X_A	O_2
2	O_3	X_B	O_4
3	O_5	X_C	O_6
4	—	X_A	O_7
5	—	X_B	O_8
6	—	X_C	O_9
7	O_{10}	—	O_{11}
8	—	—	O_{12}

Time ▶

Example for Diagram 6.3

McCarthy, A. M., & Tucker, M. L. (2002). Encouraging community service through service learning. *Journal of Management Education, 26*(6), 629–647.

Research Questions

- *Main effect:* Does the participation in a service-learning project affect a student's intention to participate in community service? Does exposure to a community-service lecture affect a student's intention to participate in community service?
- *Interaction effect:* Was there an interaction effect between the service-learning project and the community-service lecture condition and the intention to participate in community service? Which of the three conditions (i.e., service learning, service lecture, or both combined) had the greatest effect on intention to participate in community service? Was there an interaction between the students' pre-intervention intention and the particular intervention they received and their postintervention intention to engage in community service?

Procedures: The sample included 437 college students enrolled in business classes at a state university. The research design employed eight groups: six treatment (two educational groups: each by themselves and in combination) and two control groups. The first treatment was a lecture by an instructor about the benefits of community service; the second treatment was a service-learning project that required students to perform tasks related to the content of the course for a local nonprofit organization. The third treatment combined both the lecture and the service learning project interventions. The dependent variable was the students' intention to participate in community service. This outcome variable was measured via a questionnaire that was administered as a pretest on the first day of class and as a posttest during the last week of class.

Design: Quasi-experimental research utilizing a between-subjects approach and a Solomon eight-group design

Recommended parametric analysis: 2- or 3-way factorial ANOVA, hierarchical multiple regression, means analysis, or maximum likelihood regression (appropriate descriptive statistics and effect-size calculations should be included).

Assignment	Group	Pretest	Treatment	Posttest
NR	1	Questionnaire	Lecture	Questionnaire
NR	2	Questionnaire	Service Learning	Questionnaire
NR	3	Questionnaire	Both	Questionnaire
NR	4	—	Lecture	Questionnaire
NR	5	—	Service Learning	Questionnaire
NR	6	—	Both	Questionnaire
NR	7	Questionnaire	—	Questionnaire
NR	8	—	—	Questionnaire
		Time ▶		

2 × 2 (n = 210)	**Independent Variable** Lecture (X_A)	
Independent Variable Pretest	Yes	No
Yes	O_2	O_{11}
No	O_7	O_{12}

2 × 2 (n = 286)	**Independent Variable** Service Learning (X_B)	
Independent Variable Pretest	Yes	No
Yes	O_4	O_{11}
No	O_8	O_{12}

2 × 2 (n = 182)	**Independent Variable** Both (X_C)	
Independent Variable Pretest	Yes	No
Yes	O_6	O_{11}
No	O_9	O_{12}

CHAPTER 7

SINGLE-CASE APPROACH

The single-case approach is often referred to as the single-participant or single-subject design. In addition, some single-case approaches utilize more than one participant ($N = 1$) and are referred to as small-n designs, but the emphasis and unit of analysis remain on the single subject (Todman & Dugard, 2001). We remain consistent with our terminology and refer to these as single-case approaches and reserve the word "design" for the specific type of design defined within the approach. A single-case approach is used to demonstrate a form of experimental control with one participant (in some instances more than one participant). As seen in within-subject and between-subject approaches, the major contingencies required to qualify as a "true" experiment are randomization of conditions to participants (i.e., counterbalancing) or random assignment of participants to conditions. However, in single-case approaches, the participant serves as his or her own control, as well as serving in the treatment during which repeated measures are taken. More specifically, each condition is held constant and the independent variable is systematically withheld and reintroduced at various intervals as a means to study the outcome.

As a reminder, the treatment is also the same as a factor or intervention, and it is the independent variable. Although there are still debates concerning the number of experimental replications required to determine causation, as well as issues related to power, single-case approaches take a unique approach to experimentation. The threats to internal validity associated with the single-case approach are similar to those found in the within-subjects approach (e.g., sequencing effects) primarily because of the issues related to collecting repeated measures. In most cases, this approach meets the critical characteristics of experimental control (see Manolov, Solanas, Bulté, & Onghena, 2010, for a review of robustness and power of randomization tests in ABAB designs).

There are many forms, variations, and names of research designs for single-case approaches. We discuss four of the major designs here, with the understanding that this is not a comprehensive coverage of all the designs developed within this approach. The primary goal of the single-case approach is to measure the dependent variable, and at the very minimum, measure it against the presence and absence of the independent variable (treatment or intervention). Therefore, the design logic of a single-case approach starts with the baseline, which is designated as "A," and then the treatment is designated as "B." See Table 7.1 for the explanation of design notations that are unique to single-case approaches.

Table 7.1 Design Notations for Single-Case Approaches

Design Notation	Design Element
A	Baseline
B	$Treatment_A$
C	$Treatment_B$
O_n	Observations

Note: An observation (O_n) indicates multiple measures within each phase.

The most basic design within this approach is the A-B design (i.e., the dependent variable is measured during the baseline and then again during the treatment). Most single-case approach designs represent some variation and extension of the A-B design. It is important to note that, in order to qualify as an experiment, a researcher would, at a minimum, need to employ an A-B-A design (i.e., this is to establish that there is indeed a functional relationship between the independent and dependent variables). There are many other variations of this design structure such as A-B-A-B, B-A-B, or A-B-C-A (C is used to represent a second treatment or independent variable). Any variation of the A-B design can be employed based solely on theoretical and logistical considerations.

When a researcher wants to study more than one treatment at a time, a multi-element design (also referred to as multitreatment or alternating-treatment designs) can be employed. This design requires rapid shifts between or within treatments to establish experimental control, and it allows an investigator to research two or more treatments (sometimes up to five or six). The third type of design within this approach is the multiple baseline design. While the A-B and multi-element require a withdrawal or reversal of conditions, the multiple baseline design requires no withdrawal or reversal (i.e., some treatments have carryover effects so withdrawal or reversal is not theoretically appropriate). Specifically, two or more baselines are established and the intervention is introduced at various points (usually across participants), but it is never removed. Most multiple baseline designs include more than one participant, but they may be used on a single participant applying the multiple baselines across multiple behaviors (as measured by the dependent variables). As previously noted, many of the single-case approach applications include more than one participant; however, each participant is analyzed individually.

Finally, there is a changing criterion design. Similar to the multiple baseline design, the changing criterion design allows for a gradual systematic manipulation of a targeted outcome and does not require a reversal or return to baseline phase as in the A-B design. This design is best applied when the researcher is interested in observing the stepwise increases of the targeted behavior.

We included three examples of the A-B design. Specifically, an A-B-A design, an A-B-A-B design, and an A-B-A-B-C-B-C design are presented. We also introduce one example of a changing criterion design and two multiple baseline designs (a 1-factor and a 2-factor design), which are forms of the basic A-B design.

The reader is referred to Dixon et al. (2009) to learn how to create graphs in Microsoft Excel for designs within the single-case approach. The reader is also referred to the following books for a comprehensive overview of single-case approaches:

Kazdin, A. E. (2010). *Single-case research designs: Methods for clinical and applied settings.* New York, NY: Oxford University Press.

Kennedy, C. H. (2005). *Single-case designs for educational research.* Boston, MA: Pearson.

O'Neill, R. E., McDonnell, J. J., Billingsley, F. F., & Jenson, W. R. (2010). *Single case research designs in educational and community settings.* Upper Saddle River, NJ: Pearson.

| Diagram 7.1 | A-B-A Design |

Case	Baseline A	Treatment B	Baseline A
1	$O_1...O_4$	$O_1...O_4$	$O_1...O_5$

Time ▶

Example for Diagram 7.1

Haydon, T., Mancil, G. R., & Van Loan, C. (2009). Using opportunities to respond in a general education classroom: A case study. *Education and Treatment of Children, 32*(2), 267–278.

Research Question: What are the effects of a choral responding procedure and increased rate of delivering questions for an elementary student identified as at risk?

Procedures: An 11-year-old African American female student was the target participant for this study ($N = 1$). She was selected based on the fact that she displayed chronic disruptive behavior and an elevated score on the Systematic Screening for Behavior Disorders. The study took place in a science classroom. The classroom was not self-contained but considered departmentalized for the particular science class. The participant was measured on three separate dependent variables: (a) disruptive behavior, (b) correct response, and (c) on-task behavior. The treatment was identified as presenting a mode of questioning called choral responding. It consisted of an increased rate of questions and varied mode of questioning. The participant was observed during a baseline period when the teacher engaged in routine classroom instruction. Next, the choral responding technique was utilized; at this time point, the participant was again assessed on the three outcome measures. Last, the class returned to a routine lecture and the participant was assessed again on the three outcome measures.

Design: Experimental research utilizing a single-case approach and an A-B-A design

Recommended statistical analysis: Time-series analysis, autocorrelation, chi-square, or descriptive statistics (frequency, duration, latency, interresponse time, and celeration)

Case	Baseline (A) Four Observations	Treatment (B) Four Observations	Baseline (A) Five Observations
1	Disruptive behavior, correct response, on-task behavior	Disruptive behavior, correct response, on-task behavior	Disruptive behavior, correct response, on-task behavior
		Time ▶	

Diagram 7.2 A-B-A-B Design

Case	Baseline A	Treatment B	Baseline A	Treatment B
1	$O_1...O_{10}$	$O_1...O_{10}$	$O_1...O_{13}$	$O_1...O_{10}$
2	$O_1...O_{10}$	$O_1...O_{10}$	$O_1...O_{13}$	$O_1...O_{10}$
3	$O_1...O_{10}$	$O_1...O_{10}$	$O_1...O_{13}$	$O_1...O_{10}$
		Time ▶		

Note: Although this example includes a total of three subjects ($N = 3$), the emphasis remains only on the single subject, and the data between cases are not aggregated.

Example for Diagram 7.2

Bernard, R. S., Cohen, L. L., & Moffett, K. (2008). A token economy for exercise adherence in pediatric cystic fibrosis: A single-subject analysis. *Journal of Pediatric Psychology, 34*(4), 354–365.

Research Question: What are the effects of a token economy on exercise adherence in children with cystic fibrosis?

Procedures: The study included three participants ($N = 3$) between the ages of 8 and 12. Initially for the baseline phase of the study, the participants were asked to complete the Children's OMNI Scale of Perceived Exertion and an exercise diary. The diary required them to track minutes of exercise per day. The treatment phase consisted of two parts, which were the training and implementation. The participants were trained how to properly exercise and ensure activity levels at an appropriate level. The token economy was built in as part of the treatment so that whenever the participants exercised they would receive a "token" (i.e., small prize or money). The participants and their parents were also properly trained on dietary needs. The parents were asked to continue with the token economy during the treatment phase for at least one week. After the treatment phase, the token economy was removed for approximately 10 days, then returned for the next week, then removed again for the final phase. The participants completed the OMNI scale and exercise diary throughout the process.

Design: Experimental research utilizing a single-case approach and an A-B-A-B design

Recommended statistical analysis: Time-series analysis, autocorrelation, chi-square, or descriptive statistics (frequency, duration, latency, interresponse time, and celeration)

Case	Baseline (A) 10 Observations	Treatment (B) ~10 Observations	Baseline (A) 13 Observations	Treatment (B) ~10 Observations
1	OMNI Scale, exercise diary	OMNI Scale, exercise diary	OMNI Scale, exercise diary	OMNI Scale, exercise diary
2	OMNI Scale, exercise diary	OMNI Scale, exercise diary	OMNI Scale, exercise diary	OMNI Scale, exercise diary
3	OMNI Scale, exercise diary	OMNI Scale, exercise diary	OMNI Scale, exercise diary	OMNI Scale, exercise diary
	Time ▶			

Diagram 7.3 A-B-A-B-C-B-C Design

Case	Baseline A	Treatment$_A$ B	Baseline A	Treatment$_A$ B	Treatment$_B$ C	Treatment$_A$ B	Treatment$_B$ C
1	O_n	O_n	O_n	O_n	O_n	O_n	O_n
2	O_n	O_n	O_n	O_n	O_n	O_n	O_n
3	O_n	O_n	O_n	O_n	O_n	O_n	O_n
	Time ▶						

Note: Each O_n represents multiple measures (observations), sometimes referred to as sessions.

Example for Diagram 7.3

Mancil, G. R., Haydon, T., & Whitby, P. (2009). Differential effects of paper and computer-assisted Social Stories™ on inappropriate behavior in children with autism. *Focus on Autism and Other Developmental Disabilities, 24*(4), 205–215.

Research Question: What are the effects of using a social story on aberrant behaviors of children diagnosed with autism?

Procedures: Three elementary students (*N* = 3) diagnosed with autism between the ages of 6 and 9 participated in this study. The behaviors that were targeted and measured were pushing, grabbing, touching, and shoving. The first intervention (Treatment$_A$) was a computer-assisted social skills training (CASST), which included a social story told using a PowerPoint format. The story was developed to address the specific needs of autistic children. The second intervention (Treatment$_B$) included the same social story, but it was presented using a paper format. For the initial baseline condition, teachers were asked to measure aberrant behaviors (e.g., pushing, grabbing) using an event-recording system. Next, the participants were introduced to the storytelling intervention using the CASST. Another baseline was measured, and then the storytelling format using CASST was again administered. Finally, the participants were exposed to the storytelling intervention with the use of paper. A return to the original intervention was presented (CASST), and then participants were again exposed to the paper storytelling intervention. Throughout the process, teachers recorded the target behavior with the event-recording system.

Design: Experimental research utilizing a single-case approach and an A-B-A-B-C-B-C design

Recommended statistical analysis: Time-series analysis, autocorrelation, chi-square, or descriptive statistics (frequency, duration, latency, interresponse time, and celeration)

Case	Baseline (A) Five Observations	Treatment$_A$ (B) Five Observations	Baseline (A) Five Observations	Treatment$_A$ (B) Six Observations	Treatment$_B$ (C) Five Observations	Treatment$_A$ (B) Six Observations	Treatment$_B$ (C) Five Observations
1	Behavior	Behavior	Behavior	Behavior	Behavior	Behavior	Behavior
2	Behavior	Behavior	Behavior	Behavior	Behavior	Behavior	Behavior
3	Behavior	Behavior	Behavior	Behavior	Behavior	Behavior	Behavior
Time ▶							

| **Diagram 7.4** | Changing Criterion Design (A-B) |

Case	Baseline A	Treatment B
1	$O_1...O_5$	$O_1...O_{20}$
2	$O_1...O_5$	$O_1...O_{20}$
3	$O_1...O_5$	$O_1...O_{20}$

Time ▶

Note: Any number of observations can be made during the treatment phase until the designated criterion is met.

Example for Diagram 7.4

Ganz, J. B., & Flores, M. M. (2009). The effectiveness of direct instruction for teaching language to children with autism spectrum disorders: Identifying material. *Journal of Autism and Developmental Disorders, 39,* 75–83.

Research Question: What are the effects of a direct instruction language program on students with autistic spectrum disorders and their oral skills?

Procedures: Three participants (M_{age} = 10.5; N = 3) diagnosed with autism participated in this study. The intervention for this study was a direct-instruction program developed from the Language for Learning Materials. The specific strand of instruction chosen was the identification of common materials. These included items such as shirts, pants, robes, napkins, and leather shoes. The researchers created language probes designed after the tasks of the direct instruction intervention in order to assess the correct identification of items developed from the differential materials. For the initial phase, baseline data were collected until each individual performed consistently. Next, the treatment phase was implemented. The treatment phase lasted at each criterion level until all three participants achieved the predetermined criterion.

Design: Quasi-experimental research utilizing a single-case approach and changing criterion design

Recommended statistical analysis: Time-series analysis, autocorrelation, chi-square, or descriptive statistics (frequency, duration, latency, interresponse time, and celeration)

Case	Baseline *(A)* 5 Observations	Treatment *(B)* 20 Observations
1	Language probe	Language probe
2	Language probe	Language probe
3	Language probe	Language probe
Time ▶		

Diagram 7.5 Multiple Baseline Design (A-B)

Case	Baseline A_1	Treatment B
1	$O_1...O_5$	$O_1...O_{24}$

Case	Baseline A_2	Treatment B
2	$O_1...O_9$	$O_1...O_{15}$

Case	Baseline A_3	Treatment B
3	$O_1...O_{13}$	$O_1...O_{16}$

Time ▶

Note: The baselines for A_1, A_2, and A_3 should vary in length. The vertical dashed line signifies the varied length for the baseline phase between cases.

Example for Diagram 7.5

Schoenfeld, N. A., & Mathur, S. R. (2009). Effects of cognitive-behavioral intervention on the school performance of students with emotional or behavioral disorders and anxiety. *Behavioral Disorders, 34*(4), 184–195.

Research Question: What are the effects of cognitive-behavioral intervention on academic engagement and anxiety in children diagnosed with emotional and behavioral disorders?

Procedures: Three students (*N* = 3) were recruited to participate in this study. Each participant attended a private school for students with emotional and behavioral disorders. Students' levels of anxiety were assessed by their teacher using the Child Symptom Inventory IV (CSI-IV). Participants' levels of academic engagement and school-appropriate behavior were also assessed as outcome measures. The intervention was the FRIENDS program, which is a cognitive-behavioral curriculum designed to help anxious children with emotional and behavioral disorders. After the initial baseline phase, each participant was exposed to the treatment twice a week in 30-minute intervals for a total of 29 sessions for each participant, including the baseline phase.

Design: Quasi-experimental research utilizing a single-case approach and a multiple baseline design

Recommended statistical analysis: Time-series analysis, autocorrelation, chi-square, or descriptive statistics (frequency, duration, latency, interresponse time, and celeration)

Case	Baseline (A) ~5 Observations	Treatment (B) ~24 Observations
1	CVI-IV, engagement, behavior	CVI-IV, engagement, behavior
Case	Baseline (A) ~9 Observations	Treatment (B) ~15 Observations
2	CVI-IV, engagement, behavior	CVI-IV, engagement, behavior
Case	Baseline (A) ~13 Observation	Treatment (B) ~16 Observations
3	CVI-IV, engagement, behavior	CVI-IV, engagement, behavior
	Time ▶	

Diagram 7.6 Multiple Baseline Design (A-B-C)

Case	Baseline A_1	Treatment$_A$ B	Treatment$_B$ C
1	$O_1...O_n$	$O_1...O_n$	$O_1...O_n$
Case	Baseline A_2	Treatment$_A$ B	Treatment$_B$ C
2	$O_1...O_n$	$O_1...O_n$	$O_1...O_n$
	Time ▶		

Note: Four cases were used in this study.

Example for Diagram 7.6

Lyon, A. R., Gershenson, R. A., Farahmand, F. K., Thaxter, P. J., Behling, S., & Budd, K. S. (2009). Effectiveness of teacher-child interaction training (TCIT) in a preschool setting. *Behavior Modification, 33*(6), 855–884.

Research Question: What is the impact of teacher-child interaction training on preschool teachers' positive attention and discipline skills as a means to enhance children's psychosocial functioning and prevent mental health problems?

Procedures: Four classrooms and 12 teachers participated in this study. There were three teachers associated with each classroom, and each classroom represented a case ($N = 4$). The study included four experimental phases: (a) baseline, (b) treatment$_A$, (c) treatment$_B$, and (d) follow-up. The first 2 to 4 weeks served as the baseline period in which teachers were observed during routine instructional activities with the use of the Dyadic Parent-Child Interaction Coding System (DPICS). Next, the child-directed interaction (CDI) program was implemented and the observations with the DPICS continued. Then, after about 10 days, the teacher-directed interaction (TDI) program was implemented. The DPICS observation continued through this phase as well. At the commencement of the CDI and TDI phases, the teachers completed a teacher satisfaction survey. Classes 1, 2, and 3 were observed a total of 28 times and then class 4 was observed a total of 31 times over the baseline and treatment phases.

Design: Experimental research utilizing a single-case approach and a multiple baseline design

Recommended statistical analysis: Time-series analysis, autocorrelation, chi-square, or descriptive statistics (frequency, duration, latency, interresponse time, and celeration)

Case	Baseline (A) ~3 Observations	Treatment (B) ~11 Observations	Treatment (C) ~10 Observations
1	DPICS	DPICS	DPICS
Case	Baseline (A) ~6 Observations	Treatment (B) ~9 Observations	Treatment (C) ~10 Observations
2	DPICS	DPICS	DPICS
Case	Baseline (A) ~9 Observations	Treatment (B) ~13 Observations	Treatment (C) ~6 Observations
3	DPICS	DPICS	DPICS
Case	Baseline (A) ~11 Observations	Treatment (B) ~13 Observations	Treatment (C) ~7 Observations
4	DPICS	DPICS	DPICS
Time ▶			

Note: Each case represented one classroom and three teachers.

PART II

Quantitative Methods for Nonexperimental Research

T his part includes two popular approaches to the quantitative method (nonexperimental only) followed by some of the associated basic designs (accompanied by brief descriptions of published studies that utilize the design). For an in-depth understanding of the application of the design, the full article can be reviewed on the companion website, *A Cross-Section of Research Articles Classified by Design: Quantitative, Qualitative, and Mixed Methods.*

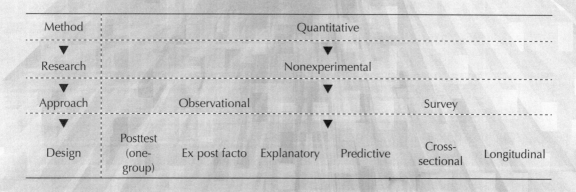

Method	Quantitative					
Research	Nonexperimental					
Approach	Observational				Survey	
Design	Posttest (one-group)	Ex post facto	Explanatory	Predictive	Cross-sectional	Longitudinal

Note: Quantitative methods for nonexperimental research are shown here followed by the approach and then the design.

95

Nonexperimental research is conducted when the researcher does not have direct control of the independent variables simply because their manifestations have already occurred. That is, nonexperimental research is utilized when the variables of interest cannot be controlled though the means of manipulation, inclusion, exclusion, or group assignment. However, the one form of control that can be utilized for nonexperimental research is through different types of statistical procedures. This form of control can include the matching or pairing of alternate forms of independent variables (e.g., gender, socioeconomic status) prior to conducting an analysis or through the application of regression-discontinuity approaches to existing data sets, causal-modeling techniques, or propensity-scoring methods (i.e., equating groups on known covariates and assigning to conditions). Although the research is considered nonexperimental, it does not imply that less value or meaning may be derived from the findings. Typically, causal relationships can only be inferred from experimental research; but considering the limitations and difficulty applying experimental research, findings from nonexperimental research (observational/correlational) can be a compelling indicator of cause and effect (e.g., the relationship between smoking cigarettes and lung cancer).

Much of our knowledge today regarding cause and effect relationships (from astronomy to epidemiology) is derived from the nonexperimental research of observational data. As previously noted, researchers believe that causal links can be drawn from examinations that are nonexperimental in nature, particularly with the application of causal-modeling techniques and propensity-scoring methods. The reader is referred to Rubin (2007, 2008) for more information regarding the approximation of observational approaches to experimental tenets. Again, in nonexperimental research, the researcher does not attempt to control or manipulate the actual conditions (i.e., independent variables); rather, control is exerted over levels of variables (through statistical procedures). Hence, technically speaking, the concept of internal validity does not apply to nonexperimental research. Nonexperimental research is primarily utilized to explain or predict relationships or to describe and measure the degree of association (relationship) among variables. However, unlike internal validity, issues related to external, construct, statistical conclusion validity should still be accounted for when conducting nonexperimental research, although these concepts were originally defined to address the issues related to the determination of cause-effect relations through experimental or quasi-experimental research.

We present a one-group posttest-only design, which is considered non-experimental and one of the "weakest" designs presented in this book. We also present one example of an ex post facto design. However, the two most common forms of quantitative methods and nonexperimental research are observational and survey approaches (sometimes referred in texts as correlational designs and descriptive research, respectively), which are presented in this part. As a simple reminder, the critical difference between experimental and nonexperimental research is the concept of control of the independent variable(s).

CHAPTER **8**

EX POST FACTO AND POSTTEST-ONLY DESIGNS

Another form of nonexperimental research is called the ex post facto (after the fact) design, sometimes referred to as causal-comparative research (the term *causal-comparative* is considered a misnomer). This widely misunderstood and underused design is an attempt at creating quasi-experimental research out of nonexperimental research. Ex post facto designs are utilized when the researcher cannot control the treatment variable (i.e., the treatment and control groups are selected after the treatment has occurred), and there are no pretest measures, while only a posttest is collected. Unlike all the designs in nonexperimental research, the ex post facto design is unique in that issues related to internal validity still should be considered when evaluating the outcomes. The major threats include history, selection bias, maturation, and attrition. Clearly, the most obvious threat is selection bias, because groups are self-selected and non-randomly assigned to conditions for a multitude of reasons. Therefore, researchers can implement some type of "control" for the selection-bias issue by utilizing a post-hoc *matched-grouping* technique. This allows the researcher to establish control over the variables of interest. That is, because the independent (treatment) variable is not manipulated, various levels of alternate independent variables (e.g., age or gender) can be statistically manipulated (controlled) and used as a means to include individuals in the desired conditions. These alternate independent variables are sometimes referred to as quasi-independent variables because they are not subjected to the various control techniques (e.g., manipulation, elimination). See Diagram 8.1 for an example of an ex post facto design. The reader is referred to Giuffre (1997) and Spector (1981) for more details regarding ex post facto designs.

Diagram 8.1 Two-Group Ex Post Facto Design

Group	Treatment	Assignment	Posttest
1	X	M_A	O_1
2	—	M_A	O_1

Time ▶

Note: M_A represents the matched-grouping criteria (i.e., statistical procedures) used as a means to include the desired participants in each condition. The assignment to conditions is conducted after the treatment has occurred.

The one-group posttest-only design (often referred to as the *one-shot case study*) is considered nonexperimental and a "weak" design. Although the one-group posttest-only design is nonexperimental, threats to internal validity still should be a consideration. That is, the major threats to internal validity associated with this design are what determine the limitations in assessing the outcome. The obvious threats are selection bias and special treatment. Because there is only one designated observation with no comparison groups or multiple observations within subjects, it is nearly impossible to rule out plausible alternative explanations (i.e., the identified cause cannot be determined to be the only explanation for the effect).

Diagram 8.2 Posttest Design (One-Group)

Group	Treatment	Posttest
1	X	O_1

Time ▶

Note: Statistical procedures is the only form of control to be utilized in nonexperimental research. However, this design is unique in that the independent variable can also be controlled via elimination and manipulation. This is the only exception in nonexperimental research.

Example for Diagram 8.2

Morgan, B. J. (2001). Evaluation of an educational intervention for military tobacco users. *Military Medicine, 166*(12), 1094–2001.

Research Question: What is the short-term effect of a tobacco-hazard education intervention on tobacco use and intent to quit?

Procedures: A tobacco-hazard education intervention was developed and presented to military tobacco users. The presentation lasted approximately 1 hour with a follow-up question and answer period. One month after the intervention, participants were asked to complete a survey regarding tobacco use and their intent to quit.

Design: Nonexperimental research utilizing a one-group posttest-only design

Recommended statistical analysis: Descriptive statistics, one-sample *t* test

Assignment	Group	Treatment	Posttest
NR	1 (*N* = 151)	Tobacco hazard education	Tobacco use, intent to quit
Time ▶			

Diagram 8.3 Ex Post Facto Design

Group	Treatment	Assignment	Group	Posttest
1	X	M_A	1	O_1
		M_A	2	O_1
		Time ▶		

Note: The current example included one treatment for both groups, but some applications of this design can include two separate treatments or a treatment and control.

Example for Diagram 8.3

Chapin, M. H., & Holbert, D. (2009). Differences in affect, life satisfaction, and depression between successfully and unsuccessfully rehabilitated persons with spinal cord injuries. *Rehabilitation Counseling Bulletin, 53*(1), 6–15.

Research Question: What are the differences between persons with spinal cord injuries who were successfully rehabilitated from those who were not in regard to affect, life satisfaction, and depression?

Procedures: A total of 67 individuals with spinal cord injuries participated in the study. The participants went through a series of rehabilitative programs from the Division of Vocational Rehabilitation Services (DVRS). Participants were then assigned (matched grouping) to conditions based on successful rehabilitation ($n = 36$) or unsuccessful rehabilitation ($n = 31$). Following the rehabilitation program, participants completed the following questionnaires: Positive and Negative Affect Scale (PANAS), Satisfaction with Life Scale (SWLS), and the Center for Epidemiological Studies-Depression Scale (CES-D).

Design: Nonexperimental research utilizing an ex post facto design

Recommended parametric analysis: ANCOVA or MANCOVA (appropriate descriptive statistics and effect-size calculations should be included).

Group	Treatment	Assignment	Group	Posttest
N = 67	DVRS program	Unsuccessful	1 (n = 31)	PANAS, SWLS, CES-D
		Successful	2 (n = 36)	PANAS, SWLS, CES-D
Time ▶				

Note: The matched-grouping assignment to each condition was based on the success of the rehabilitation program. However, for example, the researcher could have matched the groups on gender and only included males in one analysis and females in the second, although this approach would require a larger sample size.

CHAPTER 9

OBSERVATIONAL
APPROACH

T he observational approach is considered a correlational approach to research. The researcher does not intervene or use experimental control (i.e., manipulation, elimination, inclusion, group or condition assignment). The only type of control that can be utilized for nonexperimental research is statistical procedures. Investigators use this approach when they are interested in measuring the degree of association (i.e., relationship) between variables or to predict some outcome (criterion) based on the predictor variable(s). Utilizing correlational analyses or regression analyses, researchers can measure the strength (magnitude) and direction of the relationship between variables or predict the influence one variable has on another. Some researchers prefer to utilize the word *explanation* instead of *prediction* (i.e., if a phenomenon can be explained, then it can be predicted, although a prediction does not infer explanation). As previously noted, results from nonexperimental observational data oftentimes can provide a strong case for making causal inferences (e.g., the systematic observation of many data points over time, indicating that texting while driving increases the likelihood of getting into an accident). However, it is important to note that scientists should be cautious when making causal inferences based on nonexperimental observational data. The two most common designs within the observational approach are explanatory and predictive designs.

EXPLANATORY DESIGN ♦

Through correlational or regression analysis, investigators attempt to *explain* the degree of association between two (or more) variables (sometimes referred to as relational research). Within this design, data are collected at one point in time (theoretically) from a single group. Data can also be collected from extant data sets (i.e., retrospective analysis); once the research questions are applied to the data, the appropriate analyses can be employed (i.e., some form of regression analysis). More advanced explanatory designs can include collecting data from multiple variables as a means to confirm the direct and indirect effects between the variables (i.e., researchers attempt to infer causation through the application of causal modeling and confirmatory factor analysis and are sometimes referred to as single-stage and multistage models). Various forms of regression such as multiple, canonical, and cluster analysis, along with structural equation modeling, are used to summarize the data from these advanced explanatory designs (see Kline, 2010, for more information on multistage models).

PREDICTIVE DESIGN ♦

The predictive design goes beyond the explanatory design in that it allows the researcher to anticipate or *predict* the outcome based on the analysis of the relationship between two or more variables. Within this design, at least one variable is indicated as the predictor variable and one variable is designated as the criterion or outcome variable. Advanced predictive designs can include multiple predictor variables, while requiring more advanced forms of regression analyses to summarize the data. *Time* is a factor built into this design, so the researcher will typically collect data on the predictor variable(s) at one point and then at a later point collect data on the criterion variable(s). Furthermore, data can be collected from extant data sets and the predictive design can thus be applied to set up the appropriate research questions and subsequent analyses, so long as the concept of time appropriately exists between the predictor and criterion variables.

The reader is referred to the following book for further details regarding correlational approaches and analyses:

Keith, T. Z. (2006). *Multiple regression and beyond.* Boston, MA: Pearson.

Diagram 9.1	Explanatory Design

Variable	Observation
1	O_1
2	O_1

Example for Diagram 9.1

Walker, C. O., & Greene, B. A. (2009). The relations between student motivational beliefs and cognitive engagement in high school. *Journal of Educational Research, 102*(6), 463–471.

Research Question: What is the association between classroom motivation variables and students' sense of belonging?

Procedures: Questionnaires were distributed to participants ($N = 249$) and completed in English classes during the middle of the term. Perceived instrumentality and self-efficacy items were taken from the Approaches to Learning Survey. Student and classroom-achievement goal orientations were measured using the Patterns of Adaptive Learning Survey. Sense of belonging was assessed using the Psychological Sense of School Membership scale.

Design: Nonexperimental research utilizing an observational approach with an explanatory design

Recommended statistical analysis: Correlational analysis

Variable	Observation
Motivation	Self-efficacy, instrumentality, goals
Sense of belonging	Sense of belonging survey

Note: Motivation = self-efficacy, perceived instrumentality, mastery goals, and performance-based goals.

Diagram 9.2	Predictive Design₁

Variable	Observation	Observation
Predictor	O_1	—
Criterion	—	O_1

Time ▶

Note: A designated period of time must elapse before data on the criterion are collected.

Example for Diagram 9.2

Erdogan, Y., Aydin, E., & Kabaca, T. (2008). Exploring the psychological predictors of programming achievement. *Journal of Instructional Psychology, 35*(3), 264–270.

Research Question: What mental factors significantly predict programming achievement?

Procedures: Forty-eight students ($N = 48$) completed four different measurement tools that served as the predictor variables: (a) KAI creativity scale, (b) Problem Solving Inventory (PSI), (c) General Skills Test Battery (GSTB), and (d) Computer Attitude Scale (CAS). The criterion variable was measured using the Programming Achievement Test (PAT) after students completed the programming language course designed to introduce them to basic concepts of structured programming.

Design: Nonexperimental research utilizing an observational approach with a predictive design.

Recommended parametric analysis: Regression analysis or discriminant analysis (appropriate descriptive statistics and effect-size calculations should be included).

Variable	*Observation*	*Observation*
Mental factors	KAI, PSI, GSTB, CAS	—
Programming achievement	—	PAT
Time ▶		

Note: Observations from time points 1 and 2 are from the same participants.

Diagram 9.3 Predictive Design$_2$

Variable	Observation	Observation	Observation	Observation	Observation	Observation
Predictor	O_1	—	O_2	—	O_3	—
Criterion	—	O_1	—	O_2	—	O_3
			Time ▶			

Example for Diagram 9.3

Hinnant, J. B., O'Brien, M., & Ghazarian, S. R. (2009). The longitudinal relations of teacher expectations to achievement in early school years. *Journal of Educational Psychology, 101*(3), 662–670.

Research Question: To what extent do factors of teacher expectations in the early school years predict future academic performance?

Procedures: Children from 10 sites were followed from first to fifth grade (N = 2,892). Two measures of children's academic abilities were collected in the spring of the children's first- (n = 966), third- (n = 971), and fifth-grade (n = 955) years: (a) teacher reports of classroom performance in reading and math and (b) children's scores on standardized measures. In the spring of the first, third, and fifth grades, children were administered two subtests from a standardized psychoeducational assessment. A discrepancy score between teacher report of child academic performance and children's observed performance on standardized tests was calculated to determine the congruency of teacher expectancy and academic performance.

Design: Nonexperimental research utilizing a correlational approach with a predictive design

Recommended parametric analysis: Regression analysis (appropriate descriptive statistics and effect-size calculations should be included).

Variable	Observation	Observation	Observation	Observation	Observation	Observation
Teacher expectations	Teacher expectancy	—	Teacher expectancy	—	Teacher expectancy	—
Child academic performance	—	Academic performance	—	Academic performance	—	Academic performance
Time ▶						

CHAPTER 10

SURVEY APPROACH

T he most common form of nonexperimental research is the survey approach (sometimes referred to as descriptive research). Typically, investigators administer a survey to a randomly selected sample of individuals or, if possible, to an entire population (see Fowler, 2009). Random selection is a critical element to survey research in that generalization (external validity) is the primary goal of the findings (i.e., external validity is the focus; internal validity does not apply). However, it must be noted that construct validity (e.g., reactivity to assessment or acquiescence response bias) and statistical conclusion validity (e.g., unreliability of measurement) do apply to the survey approach. Again, the concept of internal validity is concerned with the establishment of cause-effect relations, whereas the survey approach is not applied to determine cause and effect. Surveys are utilized to observe trends, attitudes, or opinions of the population of interest. Participants are usually selected from the population to discover the relative incidence, distribution, and interrelations of educational, sociological, behavioral, or psychological variables. Thus, it can be classified as quantitative and is often considered a variation of the observational approach. It is important to note that some form of a probability sampling strategy (e.g., adaptive- or emergent-sampling techniques) should be employed when applying the survey approach. The reader is referred to Lavrakas (2009) for an in-depth and comprehensive coverage of the survey approach.

◆ CROSS-SECTIONAL DESIGN

The cross-sectional design allows the researcher to collect data at one point in time. This design is one of the most common designs that media outlets use to present information of public opinion on political or social circumstances. The most common application of this design is to gather opinions or attitudes from one specific group. However, in many cases the same instrument can be administered to different populations as a means to compare a group's attitudes or opinions on the same variable. Basic descriptive statistical analyses are typically used to summarize data.

◆ LONGITUDINAL DESIGN

An extension of the cross-sectional design is the longitudinal design. This design allows the researcher to collect survey data over a designated period of time with the same or different samples within a population. Researchers can collect data using *trend* (identify a population to examine changes over time), *cohort* (identify a subpopulation based on specific characteristics), or *panel* (survey the same people over time) studies. Based on theoretical and logistical considerations, longitudinal designs can include any combination of data collected from cohorts, trends, and panels. Variations of this design include the *cohort-sequential design* and the *accelerated longitudinal design*. These designs allow the researcher to collect data from temporally related cohorts over time to determine the extent of the relation between the cohorts (see Prinzie & Onghena, 2005).

The reader is referred to the following book for further details regarding survey approaches:

Fink, A. G. (2009). *How to conduct surveys: A step-by-step guide* (4th ed.). Thousand Oaks, CA: Sage.

Example for Diagram 10.1

Diagram 10.1	Cross-Sectional Design
Variable	Observation
1	O_1

Jones, M. A., Stratten, G., Reilly, T., & Unnithan, V. B. (2004). A school-based survey of recurrent non-specific low-back pain prevalence and consequences in children. *Health Education Research, 19*(3), 284–289.

Research Question: What evidence exists to demonstrate the prevalence and consequences of recurrent low-back pain in children?

Procedures: Questionnaires were issued to seven different schools ($N = 500$). A cross-sectional sample of 500 participants, boys ($n = 249$) and girls ($n = 251$), was collected. Participants were required to complete a questionnaire to assess their low-back pain history. The questionnaire was designed to identify lifetime prevalence, point prevalence, recurrent prevalence, and duration of the low-back pain.

Design: Nonexperimental research utilizing a survey approach with a cross-sectional design

Variable	Observations
Low-back pain	Low-back pain survey

Recommended statistical analysis: Descriptive statistics

Diagram 10.2 Longitudinal Design

Variable	Observation	Observation	Observation	Observation
1	O_1	O_2	O_3	O_4
2	O_1	O_2	O_3	O_4
3	O_1	O_2	O_3	O_4
4	O_1	O_2	O_3	O_4
5	O_1	O_2	O_3	O_4

Time ▶

Note: Any number of variables and observations can be associated with this design.

Example for Diagram 10.2

Steinfield, C., Ellison, N. B., & Lampe, C. (2008). Social capital, self-esteem, and use of online social network sites: A longitudinal analysis. *Journal of Applied Developmental Psychology, 29,* 434–445.

Research Questions: How does the use of a social network among a college population change over time? What is the directionality of the relationship between social network use and development of bridging social capital? How does an individual's psychological well-being influence the relationship between social capital and social network site use?

Procedures: Survey data were collected from university students at two time points a year for two consecutive years. Initially, undergraduate students were sent an e-mail invitation, with a short description of the study, information about confidentiality, an incentive for participation, and a link to the survey. Participants were surveyed on general Internet use, social network use, psychological well-being, self-esteem, and satisfaction. As a follow-up to the first-year survey, in-depth interviews were conducted with 18 students primarily drawn from the initial sample.

Design: Nonexperimental research utilizing a survey approach with a longitudinal design

Recommended parametric analysis: Descriptive statistics or correlational analysis

| Variable | *Observation* | *Observation* | *Observation* | *Observation* |
	Full Sample ($n = 288$)	*Panel* ($n = 92$)	*Random Sample* ($n = 481$)	*Panel* ($n = 92$)
Internet use	Internet use survey	Internet use survey	Internet use survey	Internet use survey
Social network use	Social network survey	Social network survey	Social network survey	Social network survey
Well-being	Well-being survey	Well-being survey	Well-being survey	Well-being survey
Self-esteem	Self-esteem survey	Self-esteem survey	Self-esteem survey	Self-esteem survey
Satisfaction	Satisfaction survey	Satisfaction survey	Satisfaction survey	Satisfaction survey
Time ▶				

Note: Panel refers to the same participants that were surveyed from the full and random samples.

PART III

Qualitative Methods

T his part includes four popular approaches to the qualitative method followed by some of the associated basic designs (accompanied by brief descriptions of published studies that utilize the design). For an in-depth understanding of the application of the design, the full article can be reviewed on the companion website, *A Cross-Section of Research Articles Classified by Design: Quantitative, Qualitative, and Mixed Methods* (http://www.sagepub.com/edmonds).

Method	Qualitative					
▼	▼					
Research	Nonexperimental					
▼	▼					
Approach	Grounded Theory	Ethnographic		Narrative		Phenomenology
▼	▼					
Design	Systematic Descriptive	Emerging Explanatory	Constructivist Existential	Realist Transcendental	Critical	Case Study Hermeneutic

Note: Qualitative methods for nonexperimental research are shown here followed by the approach and then the design.

The qualitative method represents a form of data collection and analysis with a focus on understanding and an emphasis on meaning. Research under the qualitative method is considered emerging and nonexperimental. This method is often used to explore the "how" and "why" of systems and human behavior and what governs these behaviors. Specifically, it is a method for examining phenomena, predominantly using "words" for data. The qualitative process is generally inductive, although it can be abductive (an inductive-deductive cycle) and emerging. Qualitative researchers usually take a naturalistic approach to the world (i.e., studying things in their natural setting), while attempting to understand phenomena through the "voice" of the participants. Biases are accepted as part of the process (e.g., purposive sampling [participant is the instrument] and data collection). Behavior is generally studied as it occurs naturally with no manipulation or control. The overarching aim of the qualitative method is to understand or interpret phenomena within the context of the meaning that people express without attempting to infer causation or generalize (i.e., external validity) the results to other individuals or populations. However, as previously mentioned, the concept of external validity can have a place in qualitative methods such as *theory-focused* and *case-to-case generalization* (see Chenail, 2010, for a review on nonprobabilistic approaches to generalizability for qualitative methods), as well as improving issues related to validity (e.g., trustworthiness) and reliability through triangulation techniques (Golafshani, 2003).

Generally, as noted earlier, the aim of the qualitative method is to reveal and understand phenomena within a particular context without attempting to infer any type of causation. That is, in order to infer cause and effect, the tenets of quantitative methods and sound experimental research must be followed; however, there is a unique technique utilized to infer causation from qualitative case studies known as *qualitative comparative analysis* (QCA). QCA, developed by Ragin (1997), allows researchers to combine the in-depth qualitative methodological strategies with a quantitative-oriented approach into a single framework. QCA is utilized when a researcher has data from a moderate number of cases (typically too many for a traditional cross-case qualitative analysis), then transcribes the data via qualitative analytic software, and converts the data to dichotomous or ordinal data in preparation for the QCA analysis. At that point, the researcher attempts to draw causal inferences from the outcomes of the QCA analysis (see Rihoux & Lobe, 2009, for more on QCA applications).

Although we include many specific (named) designs utilized by qualitative researchers, it is important to discuss what we refer to as the *generic* qualitative design. The generic design for qualitative methods can borrow from any of the approaches and designs covered in this section. The generic design is a "catch all" approach, with qualitative data analyses being the common thread between the various manifestations. This type of analysis is primarily an inductive process (or abductive) involving the organization of data into categories and the subsequent identification of patterns and relationships among these categories. Although the approach to data collection and analytic style differ among these generic designs, the general process of qualitative data analysis is fairly standard (see Wertz, Charmaz, McMullen, Josselson, Anderson, & Emalinda, 2011).

THE CASE STUDY ♦

Many disciplines utilize various forms of the case study to examine an individual or phenomenon within a specified context. The approach and application of case study designs also can vary widely between various disciplines such as medicine, law, and the social sciences. However, in the social and behavioral sciences, case studies are often referred to as uncontrolled studies. Yin (2009) defined the case study as an empirical inquiry that investigates a phenomenon within its real-world context, when the boundaries between phenomena and context are not clearly evident, in which multiple data sources are used. Yin referred to the case study as a "method" as opposed to confining it to only an approach or a "tradition" within the various forms of qualitative research (e.g., Creswell, 2007). Generally, the focus of the case study is on developing a narrative or revealing a phenomenon based on an in-depth, real-time, or retrospective analysis of a case. Therefore, issues related to experimental control and internal validity are nonfactors within this approach. Although case studies do not infer causation and the results cannot be generalized, the findings can provide rich insight toward phenomena and serve as support for theories and the generation of hypotheses. However, if desired, Yin does offer approaches and models for researchers interested in attempting to infer causation from case study designs (which differs from QCA analysis).

The emphasis in a case study is primarily the qualitative method; however, cross sections of quantitative data are usually collected as supplementary data throughout the analyses (see mixed-method embedded case study design). It is important to note that the label of "case study" is often applied to many social science examinations as a catchall term, many times misapplying the concept (Malcolm, 2010). However, the case study design can be applied to any of the approaches within the qualitative method, such as the most commonly applied narrative and phenomenological approach in psychology (Singer & Bonalume, 2010a) or the ethnographic approach in education

(Creswell, 2012). Creswell took a different angle than Yin (2009) regarding the type and description of designs for the case study. Gall, Gall, and Borg (2007) succinctly described a case study "as (a) the in-depth study of (b) one or more instances of a phenomenon (c) in its real-life context that (d) reflects the perspective of the participants involved in the phenomenon" (p. 447). Confusion does arise when authors utilize different terminology for similar constructs between texts. For example, Yin uniquely defined and applied the terms "holistic" and "embedded" differently than their traditional uses; for example, the term *embedded* has an entirely different meaning when used with mixed methods. As previously noted, the case study design is often used within the qualitative method and often with the ethnographic and phenomenological approaches. However, the case study can be applied to the narrative approach and arguably any other approach within the qualitative method, as long as the "case" being explored is bound by time, place, person, or environment. We refer the reader to Yin's (2004, 2009, 2012) books for a review of his unique and widely accepted approach to the case study. See Appendix B for a list of case study designs defined by Yin (2009) and Creswell (2012).

Recommended programs for qualitative data analyses: ATLAS/TI, The Ethonograph, HyperRESEARCH, NVivo, NUD?IST, SPSS Text Analysis for Surveys™

The reader is referred to the following books and book chapter for further details regarding qualitative methods:

Creswell, J. W. (2007). *Qualitative inquiry and research design: Choosing among five approaches* (2nd ed.). Thousand Oaks, CA: Sage.

Guba, E. G., & Lincoln, Y. S. (2005). Paradigmatic controversies, contradictions, and emerging influences. In N. K. Denzin & Y. S. Lincoln (Eds.), *The Sage handbook of qualitative research* (3rd ed.), pp. 191–215. Thousand Oaks, CA: Sage.

Wertz, F. J., Charmaz, K., McMullen, L. M., Josselson, R., Anderson, R., & Emalinda, M. (2011). *Five ways of doing qualitative analysis: Phenomenological psychology, grounded theory, discourse analysis, narrative research, and intuitive inquiry.* New York, NY: Guilford Press.

CHAPTER 11

GROUNDED THEORY APPROACH

The grounded theory approach was first developed by Glaser and Strauss (1967) as a way to generate a theory based on data that are systematically gathered and analyzed. In general, this is an inductive process where the theoretical propositions are not presented a priori; rather, the theory emerges from the data that are being collected. However, this process often becomes abductive, with testing of the theory occurring as it emerges from the data. The emerging theory is constantly being compared to the evidence brought forth from new data that are analyzed, as in the "constant comparative method." The use of *memoing* (i.e., the process of recording the personal thoughts and ideas of the researcher throughout the data collection procedures) is critical when using a systematic, emerging, or constructivist design. Qualitative researchers often use memoing to help make conceptual links between raw data and abstractions to better explain the phenomena being studied within its appropriate context. See Birks, Chapman, and Francis (2008) for an in-depth discussion of memo-writing techniques.

According to Corbin and Strauss (2007), a good grounded theory should (a) fit the phenomenon; (b) provide understanding; (c) provide generality, in that the theory includes extensive variation and is abstract enough to be applicable to a wide variety of contexts; and (d) provide control, in the sense of stating the conditions under which the theory applies and describing a reasonable basis for action.

♦ SYSTEMATIC DESIGN

The systematic design is the most structured of the grounded theory approaches, with rigid procedures and a preconceived framework for categories. This design emphasizes theory verification based on the theory that is generated (i.e., inductive-deductive process). The design uses the three-stage coding method (open, axial, and selective) to help generate a visual depiction of a theory.

♦ EMERGING DESIGN

The emerging design is also a theory generation design; however, it is less prescriptive than the systematic design. This design allows the theory to emerge "naturally" from the data. The key components of this design are fit, work, relevance, and modifiability.

♦ CONSTRUCTIVIST DESIGN

The constructivist design further distances itself from the procedurally laden systematic design, stressing the role of the researcher as an active participant who interacts with the field being explored. Constructivist researchers are interested in the co-construction of knowledge between researcher and participant and embrace and explore the inherent biases within this interaction. This design recognizes that knowledge emerging from the data is not only "discovered" but also created. It is important to be cognizant of the assumptions brought to the investigation by the researcher. Also, one should be aware of the socially constructed meanings that occur during the collection of data and those socially constructed meanings that were in place prior to engaging with the participant.

WHEN TO USE GROUNDED THEORY

- To build/discover theory inductively
- To build/discover substantive and/or formal theory
- When there is little or no prior information on an area or phenomenon
- To study the microcosm of interaction

The reader is referred to the following books for further details regarding the grounded theory approach:

Charmaz, K. (2006). *Constructing grounded theory: A practical guide through qualitative analysis.* London, England: Sage.

Glaser, B. G., & Strauss, A. (1967). *The discovery of grounded theory: Strategies for qualitative research.* Hawthorne, NY: Aldine Transaction.

Corbin, J., & Strauss, A. (2007). *Basics of qualitative research: Techniques and procedures for developing grounded theory* (3rd ed.). Thousand Oaks, CA: Sage.

Figure 11.1 Systematic Design

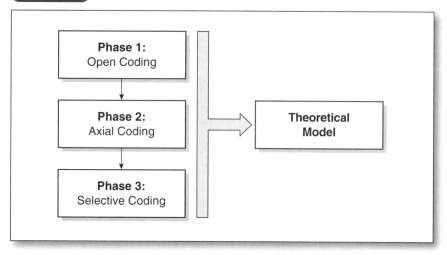

Example for Figure 11.1

Han, G. S., & Davies, C. (2006). Ethnicity, health and medical care: Towards a critical realist analysis of general practice in the Korean community in Sydney. *Ethnicity and Health, 11*(4), 409–430.

Research Question: What are the general practitioners' views on the health of Koreans and the complex process of providing and seeking effective and satisfactory medical care?

Procedures: This study investigated the use and provision of biomedicine among men on the basis of interview data from eight doctors. Semistructured interview schedules were prepared around the doctors' views of (a) health, immigrant life, and healthcare use among Koreans from different socio-economic backgrounds; (b) common ailments; (c) particular difficulties servicing fellow Koreans; (d) general practitioner referrals to specialists; and (e) the competing nature of doctoring. The interviews with the eight doctors were tape-recorded and then transcribed into a full-text report for analysis.

First, *open coding* of the data was conducted to form categories of information about the event being examined. Next, *axial coding* was performed; this step involved the researchers taking one of the categories generated during open coding and exploring it as a core phenomenon. During this phase, other categories (e.g., casual conditions, content, intervening condition, strategies, and consequences) were connected to the core phenomenon. Finally, in *selective coding*, the core category (i.e., the central phenomenon under investigation) was selected and systematically related (or integrated) with other categories. These three phases allowed for the construction of the overarching theoretical model.

Design: Qualitative method utilizing a grounded theory approach with a systematic design.[1]

Figure 11.2 Emerging Design

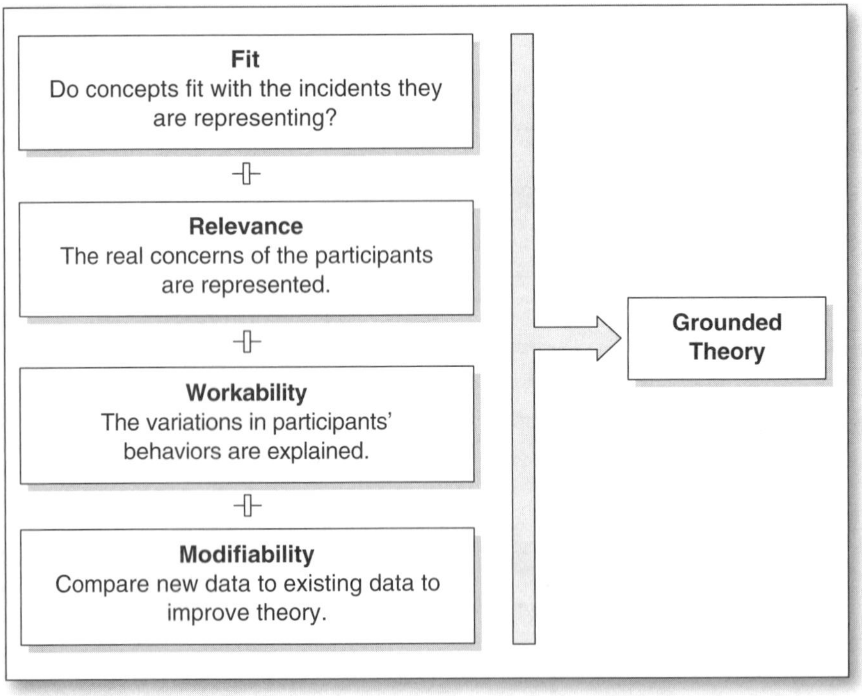

Source: Glaser and Strauss (1967).

---

[1]Although the authors state a "critical realist analysis" in the title, a systematic design was applied.

Example for Figure 11.2

Zoffmann, V., & Kirkevold, M. (2007). Relationships and their potential for change developed in difficult type 1 diabetes. *Qualitative Health Research, 17*(5), 625–638.

Research Aim: To develop a theory that interprets patient-provider relationships as a framework for acknowledging and exploiting the relational potential for change in difficult diabetes care.

Procedures: Dyads (one patient and one nurse) were formed based on the assignment of nurses to patients in the units. Following the principles of theoretical sampling, researchers used the first case (dyad) to generate a hypothesis. To investigate and compare the processes related to this hypothesis, subsequent patients were theoretically sampled to ensure a variation in levels of self-management resources. As the primary data sources, two patient-nurse conversations were taped from each dyad, one at the beginning and one at the end of the hospital stay. These interviews revealed the experiences, considerations, and feelings of both parties with regard to the hospital stay.

The abductive process of applying constant comparative analysis was performed. First, initial open coding of each interview was conducted. Through a combination of listening and writing, notes were created that provided ideas for the tentative advancement of more abstract codes. Second, critical comparisons were performed on the most solid categories that were supported by transcriptions of the coded data. This process was used to specify the content and further the advancement of lasting categories and subcategories. During the third step, comparisons across data sources were performed to explore and confirm links between concepts and thus pattern out theoretical connections. These initial theoretical constituents were compared in the fourth step (ongoing throughout the process of writing) to connect them to larger elements for further theory building. At each step, there was a return to former steps to test fit, work, relevance, and modifiability.

Design: Qualitative method utilizing a grounded theory approach with an emerging design

Figure 11.3   Constructivist Design

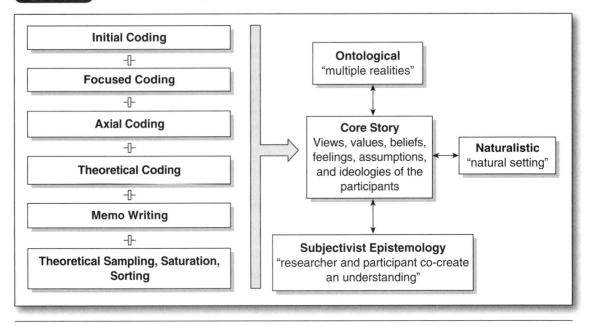

Source: Charmaz (2006).

Example for Figure 11.3

Jones, S. R., & Hill, K. E. (2003). Understanding patterns of commitment: Student motivation for community service involvement. *Journal of Higher Education, 74*(5), 516–539.

Guiding Research Questions: What are students' reasons for participation in community service in high school? What are students' reasons for participation in community service (or not) in college? How do students explain and understand the relationship between high school and college involvement? To what extent do students attribute differences or changes in their motivations as well as to their experiences?

Procedures: Purposeful sampling was used for both the identification of college and university participants and the selection of student participants at each institution. The primary strategy for data collection was in-depth, semistructured interviewing. Questions focused on the nature of community service involvement in high school and college, the reasons students attributed to their participation, and the meaning they attached to community service. The researchers were also interested in understanding the campus context in which students' decisions about community service participation were enacted. Thus, they examined materials from the community service programs.

All data were analyzed using the *constant comparative method.* The analytic process moves from more concrete codes to abstract themes and categories that are reflective of the meaning that participants attach to their experiences, rather than the generation of objective truth. Thus, the data analysis proceeds in a cyclical manner with the researchers constantly returning to the data with new questions and ideas until a narrative emerges that describes the essence of experience for study participants. This essence of experience is described as the core story.

Design: Qualitative method utilizing a grounded theory approach with a constructivist design

CHAPTER 12

ETHNOGRAPHIC APPROACH

E thnography is an approach that was developed to describe cultures; this includes any culture that shares group characteristics such as values, beliefs, or ideas. The ethnographic researcher is interested in understanding another way of life from the point of view of the participants who make up the culture or group being studied. Because this approach is based on understanding anything associated with human behavior and belief, it is well-suited for the fields of education and the social and behavioral sciences.

Ethnography can be defined as research designed to describe and analyze the social life and culture of a particular social system, based on detailed observations of what people actually do. The researcher is embedded within the culture and takes a firsthand account of the beliefs, motivations, and behaviors of the individuals in the group. The data that are collected are used to (a) document the lives of the participants within the context of the culture, (b) understand the experiences of the individuals within the culture, or (c) interpret the behaviors shaped by the cultural context.

◆ REALIST DESIGN

Van Maanen (1988) stressed three aspects of the realist design: (a) the invisible author (i.e., narrating in third person), (b) thick descriptions of the mundane (using a system of standard categories to organize the descriptions), and

(c) interpretive "omnipotence" (i.e., allowing the author the final word in presenting the culture). The realist design offers one researcher's overall perspective of a phenomenon from facts that are meticulously culled down to support a perspective. Thus, although the researcher's duty is to objectively (without bias) present the facts, ultimately the interpretations of the facts come from the "omnipotent" researcher. In general, Spradley's (1979, 1980) designs are less "narrative" or "literary" than those of Van Maanen (1988) and Geertz (1998).

CRITICAL DESIGN ◆

The critical design allows for the critiquing (i.e., challenging the status quo) of some existing system while maintaining a level of scientific inquiry. It provides a scientific framework for advocacy or a structure for directly examining relationships among cultural features, economic systems, knowledge, society, and political action. Put simply, Madison (2005) and Thomas (1993) both asserted that the critical design is used to describe, analyze, and scrutinize hidden agendas, power centers, and assumptions that inhibit, repress, and constrain. Thus, the real utility of a critical design is the structure it provides for researchers who are interested in explaining some form of ideology or power relations through the transformation of meaning and conceptualization of existing social systems.

CASE STUDY DESIGN ◆

The case study design is often used with the ethnographic approach; however, it has some distinct differences from traditional ethnography. While traditional ethnography is focused on group behavior, the case study design allows for the investigation of individuals as a whole (Creswell, 2012).[1] This design provides the framework for an in-depth contextual analysis of a finite number of events or conditions and their associations. More specifically, the ethnographic case study allows for the examination of an actual case within some cultural group. The "case" being explored also can be a group bounded by time, place, or environment (i.e., a group must be considered a unit, which is more than just a homogenous group). Researchers interested in exploring activities of a group, rather than shared patterns of group behavior, should follow this design.

---

[1]Creswell (2012) identified many different types of designs within the ethnographic approach such as confessional, life history, autoethnography, microethnography, feminist, postmodern, and ethnographic novels.

WHEN TO USE ETHNOGRAPHY

- Studying a school, organization, or program in-depth
- Studying what people do
- Studying how things work or run
- Studying "insiders"
- Studying aspects of "culture" (e.g., practices, rituals, lives, inter-connections, customs, values, beliefs, everyday life)

The reader is referred to the following books for further details regarding the ethnographic approach:

Fetterman, D. M. (2009). *Ethnography: Step-by-step* (3rd ed.). Thousand Oaks, CA: Sage.

Madison, D. S. (2005). *Critical ethnography: Methods, ethics, and performance*. Thousand Oaks, CA: Sage.

Figure 12.1 Realist Design

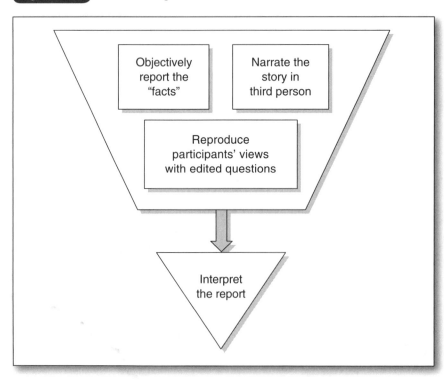

Makagon, D., & Neumann, M. (2009). *Recording culture.* Thousand Oaks, CA: Sage.

Van Maanen, J. (1988). *Tales of the field: On writing ethnography.* Chicago, IL: University of Chicago Press.

Example for Figure 12.1

Purser, G. (2009). The dignity of job-seeking men: Boundary work among immigrant day laborers. *Journal of Contemporary Ethnography, 38*(1), 117–139.

Research Aim: Examine the discourses through which Latino immigrant day laborers make sense of, and find dignity within, their ongoing quest for work.

Procedures: The data collection involved ethnographic fieldwork and interviews with individual day laborers. The researcher conducted a total of 22 in-depth, loosely structured interviews with day laborers, 10 of whom regularly sought work out of the center and 12 of whom regularly sought work on the street. This was followed by a series of open-ended questions that focused on the objective and subjective dimensions of the men's work experiences and job-searching strategies. Substantial attention was devoted to understanding how the men made sense of their precarious position on the margins of the labor market.

This study involved an inductive approach to data analysis. The third-person voice was used, and no personal ideas were included in the report; rather, the facts were presented through the actual words of the participants. Objective data were reported without personal bias or judgment. Ordinary details of each participant's life were included, and standard categories for cultural description were used (e.g., work life and family systems). The final interpretive report allowed the researcher to provide subjective explanations of the data representing the culture being studied.

Design: Qualitative method utilizing an ethnographic approach with a realist design

Figure 12.2 Critical Design

Collaborate with participants to prevent further marginalization (give back to the participants studied)	Empower participants through "speaking" on their behalf (nonneutral stance)

Goal
To change societal views or challenge the status quo

Embrace biases in research (researcher's role is reflexive and self-aware)	Connect the meaning of a situation to the broader context of social issues

Example for Figure 12.2

Varcoe, C., Browne, A. J., Wong, S., & Smye, V. L. (2009). Harms and benefits: Collecting ethnicity data in a clinical context. *Social Science & Medicine, 68,* 1659–1666.

Research Aim: Critically examine the implications of collecting ethnicity data in healthcare settings.

Procedures: Data were collected in four modes: (a) in-depth interviews with decision makers and policy leaders affiliated with health authorities, (b) focus groups of community leaders who served on committees of the health authority to represent patients' perspectives concerning healthcare planning, (c) semistructured interviews with patients seeking health services in either a subacute area or a community health center, and (d) interviews with healthcare workers who were involved in either administering an ethnic identity question in healthcare agencies or whose agencies were considering doing so as part of intake data. Patient interviews were focused on their thoughts of their identification of ethnicity in healthcare settings, past experiences with being asked, and their thoughts on the benefits and concerns.

An interpretive thematic analysis was conducted. The theoretical perspective was guided by an ethical lens. Each transcript and associated field notes were read to get a sense of the whole and then coded thematically. Collaboration with participants occurred throughout the process to optimize the study's benefits and avoid harm. The meaning of the phenomenon under investigation was connected

Figure 12.3 Case Study Design

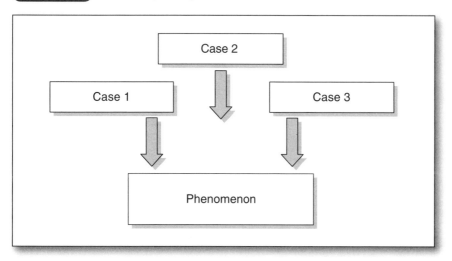

to the broader context of power and the social positions of patients within existing power structures. Themes were compared across interviews and revised based upon the views and biases of the researcher and participants. The final report advocated on behalf of the participant group. The researchers challenged the status quo assumption that providing quality care in the clinical context requires the collection of ethnicity data. The intent was to change societal standards by a call to action and to address the structural inequities at healthcare settings.

Design: Qualitative method utilizing an ethnographic approach with a critical design

Example for Figure 12.3[2]

Richardson, J. B. (2009). Men do matter: Ethnographic insights on the socially supportive role of the African American uncle in the lives of inner-city African American male youth. *Journal of Family Issues, 30*(8), 1041–1069.

Research Question: What is the role of the African American uncle as a form of social support and social capital in the lives of adolescent African American males living in single-female-headed households?

---

[2]According to Creswell (2012), this example is a collective case study, with several (there can be more than three) cases that provide insight into a phenomenon. There is also an (a) intrinsic case study design, which explores a single unusual case; and (b) an instrumental case study design, which examines a single case to gain insight into a phenomenon.

Procedures: The study involved in-depth life-history interviews and ethnographic participant observations of young men and their single mothers over a period of four years. The use of ethnography provided exhaustive and rich contextual data. The qualitative inquiry highlights the contextual nature of social life; it explores subjective perceptions and meanings, and it identifies social processes and dynamics. In the three cases studied, the young men in the sample and their mothers were able to clearly identify and explain the socially supportive role that uncles filled as surrogate fathers. In some instances, the uncles themselves articulated their roles as surrogate fathers.

First, a phenomenon (role of the African American uncle as a form of social support) was identified. Next, the appropriate case(s) (individual, activity, event, or process) were chosen that allowed for the examination of the phenomenon. The description and comparisons of three cases helped to provide insight into the role of the African American uncle as a form of social support in the lives of adolescent African American males (i.e., the phenomenon). Multiple forms of data were collected to increase the depth of understanding regarding the phenomenon of interest. The cases were also presented within a larger context (setting, political climate, social and economic status).

Design: Qualitative method utilizing an ethnographic approach with a case study design

CHAPTER 13

NARRATIVE APPROACH

T he narrative approach involves gathering information, in the form of storytelling of the participant, for the purpose of understanding a phenomenon. Humans are storytelling beings by nature; we lead storied lives, both individually and collectively. Ultimately, the narrative approach is most widely used in the disciplines of psychology and psychiatry and is the study of the multitude of ways humans experience the world. Specifically, this approach involves collaboration between the researcher and participant, as a way to understand phenomena through stories lived and told. The narrative design involves (a) the exploration of a single participant or a small sample of participants, (b) gathering data through the collection of stories, (c) retelling the stories (restorying), and (d) reviewing the story with the participant to help validate the meaning and subsequent interpretation. The narrative design can be either biographical or autobiographical.

Dialogic listening skills are essential to the narrative approach; this type of "listening" is used throughout the whole process, as the researcher gathers data through conversations and engaged interchanges of ideas and information with the participant(s). The narrative approach can be conceptualized as descriptive, explanatory, or critical by design and follows the "underlying assumptions that there is neither a single, absolute truth in human reality nor one correct reading or interpretation of a text" (Polkinghorne, 1988, p. 2). There is also a structural approach in the way individual's stories are studied (Riessman, 2007).

Dan McAdams (creating self in narrative) and Jefferson Singer (explanatory potential of the life story) have had a profound influence on the development and use of the narrative approach within the social and behavioral sciences. McAdams, Josselson, and Lieblich's (2006) contributions included (a) the Life Story Interview method, (b) the Guided Autobiography, (c) the Loyola Generativity Scale, and (d) a set of coding manuals to analyze the stories of research participants. Singer's (1997) book, *Message in a Bottle,* focused on men whose addictions were resistant to the traditional 12-step method and served as an excellent exemplar of the narrative approach. Singer also utilized the explanatory potential of the life story of individuals within the therapeutic context (see Singer & Bonalume, 2010a and 2010b, for more on autobiographical narrative approaches for case studies in psychotherapy).

◆ DESCRIPTIVE DESIGN

The descriptive design involves the description of any one or more of the following: (a) individual or group narratives of life stories or specific life events, (b) the conditions or contextual factors supporting the story, (c) the relationship between individual stories and the culture the stories are embedded within, and (d) how certain life events impact the participant's story line. Thus, the descriptive design is used to explore the status of some phenomenon and to describe what exists with respect to the individual, group, or condition.

◆ EXPLANATORY DESIGN

The explanatory design is used to provide an account of some phenomenon by means of why something happened. Thus, the explanatory design is used to explore the causes and reasons of phenomena.

◆ CRITICAL DESIGN

Van Maanen (1988), in his book on ethnography, discussed the use of "critical tales." These critical tales are conceptualized as narrative approaches using a critical framework. A critical tale may illuminate individual experiences as well as larger social, political, symbolic, or economic issues. Thus, the critical design within the narrative approach involves the same structure or framework as the critical design within the ethnographic approach. Ultimately, this design allows for the critiquing of some existing system while maintaining a level of scientific inquiry.

WHEN TO USE NARRATIVE INQUIRY

- Telling stories about stories
- Exploring identity and conflict
- Examining the structure of experience
- Focusing on how people create meaning in their lives
- Exploring the interaction of individual stories with cultural narratives

The reader is referred to the following books for further details regarding the narrative approach:

Clandinin, D. J., & Connelly, F. M. (2000). *Narrative inquiry: Experience and story in qualitative research.* San Francisco, CA: Wiley.

Lieblich, A., Tuval-Mashiach, R., & Zilber, T. (1998). *Narrative research: Reading, analysis, and interpretation.* Thousand Oaks, CA: Sage.

Riessman, C. K. (2007). *Narrative methods for the human sciences.* Thousand Oaks, CA: Sage.

Figure 13.1   Descriptive Design

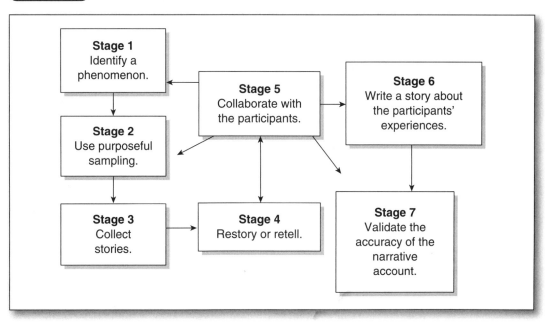

Note: At Stage 5 of the process the researcher can revert back to any previous stage as indicated by the arrows.

Example for Figure 13.1

Lapadat, J. C. (2004). Autobiographical memories of early language and literacy development. *Narrative Inquiry, 14*(1), 113–140.

Research Aim: To explore adults' memories of their own acquisition of language and literacy learning

Procedures: Participants kept a journal in which they made regular entries over the semester reflecting on their own personal history of learning language and literacy from the preschool years through the end of adolescence. The participants were asked to recall personally significant events, situations, and people that made a difference to their learning, as well as ways in which their learning and use of language made a difference in their lives. The participants were asked to structure entries around particular topics they set for themselves, to avoid holding tightly to a chronological sequence, and to discuss specific examples.

In Stage 1, the researchers chose to explore the acquisition of early language and literacy. Purposeful sampling (Stage 2) was conducted (i.e., adults in a language development seminar). During Stage 3, stories from the participants were collected (e.g., personal history of learning language and literacy). The fourth stage involved the identification of categories (e.g., family and home, peers and friends, school and teachers, books and becoming literate, culture and languages) and then *restorying* by sequencing and organizing the elements of the story identified by the researcher (e.g., poetic transcription). The fifth stage occurred throughout the process, as the researcher collaborated with the participant to ensure the validity of the individual experiences. Stage 6 involved the use of the first person to complete the narrative report. During Stage 7, the researcher consulted with the participants to ensure the accuracy of the final narrative account.

Design: Qualitative method utilizing a narrative approach with a descriptive design

Example for Figure 13.2

Hirakata, P. (2009). Narratives of dissociation: Insights into the treatment of dissociation in individuals who were sexually abused as children. *Journal of Trauma & Dissociation, 10*(1), 297–314.

Figure 13.2 Explanatory Design

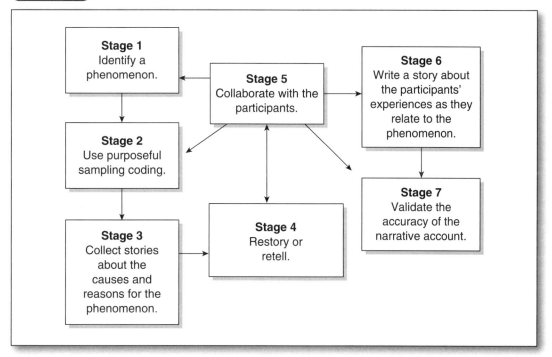

Research Aim: To explore the treatment of dissociation and provide support for treatment approaches that are viewed as helpful by clients who engage in dissociative behavior

Procedures: Participants engaged in a single interview (cross-sectional) designed to identify factors that positively or negatively influenced therapy and minimized the overall need to dissociate. Interviews were semistructured and included questions such as "How was dissociation addressed in therapy?" "What did you find helpful?" and "What did you find not helpful or even harmful?" The interviews were also audiotaped and transcribed and the data were analyzed using a holistic-content approach (Lieblich, Tuval-Mashiach, & Zilber, 1998): Each interview was read for its content in a holistic manner until patterns, or themes, began to emerge. Global impressions were noted by the space dedicated to a certain issue and the repetitive nature that occurred both within and across narratives. Any exceptions or unusual and contradictory features were also recognized. Each participant read and validated his or her individual narrative.

Three major themes emerged from this study: (a) tools and techniques, (b) a nonpathologizing approach, and (c) the therapeutic relationship. These themes were further divided into 16 subthemes. Each subtheme was discussed individually, and excerpts from the participants' interviews were provided. The findings from this study were explanatory in nature, providing insight into the treatment of dissociation.

Design: Qualitative method utilizing a narrative approach with an explanatory design

Figure 13.3 Critical Design

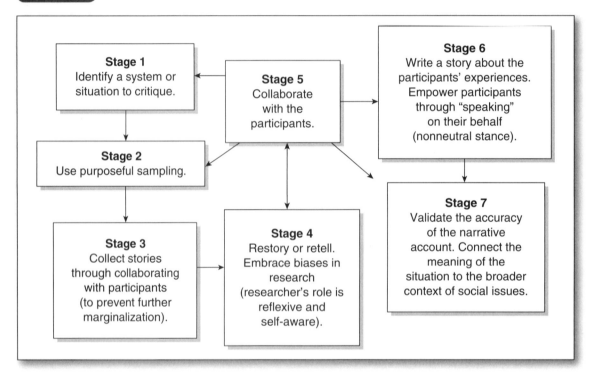

Example for Figure 13.3

Berman, H., Mulcachy, G. A., Forchuk, C., Edmunds, K. A., Haldenby, A., & Lopez, R. (2009). Uprooted and displaced: A critical narrative study of homeless, aboriginal, and newcomer girls in Canada. *Issues in Mental Health Nursing, 30*(7), 418–430.

Research Aim: Examine how uprooting and displacement have shaped mental health among three groups: (a) newcomers to Canada (immigrant and refugee girls), (b) homeless girls, and (c) Aboriginal girls.

Procedures: During face-to-face dialogic interviews, the researchers explored the means and strategies of uprooting and displacement and how these experiences affected the participants. Dialogic and reflective techniques were used to allow the respondents to become actively involved in the construction and validation of meaning (Maguire, 1987). An interview guide was used flexibly, with probes to encourage dialogue, critical reflection, and elaboration of responses. The research team was there to establish the context for the interview, offering overall direction and providing affirming feedback. However, the open-ended structure to the narrative interview allowed the participants to direct the flow and focus of the conversation.

All participants were given the choice of being interviewed alone or in a small group consisting of two to four girls. The researcher's rationale for this option was the potential power of group interviews to provide a context in which individuals are able to analyze the struggles they had encountered and the challenges they had faced, to simultaneously begin to collectivize their experiences, and to develop a sense of empowerment as they began to see the possibilities for change. The researchers analyzed the participants' words systematically, in line with the narrative approach.

The researchers were guided by the supposition that the stories told by participants would provide insight into the perceptions about what happened to them, as well as the social, economic, and political meanings of those events. Consistent with the tenets of a critical design, the researcher's goal was to facilitate the development of knowledge in ways that had the potential for emancipation and empowerment.

Design: Qualitative method utilizing a narrative approach with a critical design

CHAPTER 14

PHENOMENOLOGICAL APPROACH

P henomenology, put simply, is the description of an individual's immediate experience. The phenomenological approach was born out of Edmond Husserl's philosophical position that the starting point for knowledge was the self's experience of phenomena, such as one's conscious perceptions and sensations that arise from life experience. From this philosophy emerged the modern-day phenomenological approach to research with the goal of understanding how individuals construct reality. Researchers use the phenomenological approach when they are interested in exploring the meaning, composition, and core of the lived experience of specific phenomena. The researcher explores the conscious experiences of an individual in an attempt to distill these experiences or get at their essence.

◆ EXISTENTIAL DESIGN

The aim is to illuminate the essential general meaning structure of a specific phenomenon, with a focus on grasping the whole meaning of the experience, instead of dividing it into parts. Researchers using the existential design move from the concrete description of the experience of a given participant (co-researcher) to the interpretation of said experience. The participants (co-researchers) are asked for a description of their concrete experiences. The ultimate goal is to comprehend human experience as it is actually lived in the "real world" rather than in some artificial environment (von Eckartsberg, 1997).

Basic themes of existential phenomenology are (a) lived experience, (b) modes of being, and (c) ontology (the study of the nature of being, existence, or reality). In fact, the existential phenomenology associated with Heidegger's philosophy is often referred to as ontological phenomenology, as it is primarily concerned with "being." This differs from transcendental phenomenology, which is most associated with Husserl's epistemological philosophy (concerned with knowledge).

TRANSCENDENTAL DESIGN ♦

Some key tenets of the transcendental design are (a) intentionality (consciousness is always intentional), (b) eidetic reduction (researcher accesses the consciousness of the participant to get at the pure essence of some phenomenon, thus revealing the essential structure), and (c) constitution of meaning (returning to the world from consciousness). This design is descriptive in nature, as it is through analysis and description of how things are constituted in, and by, consciousness that allows us to understand various phenomena. This design is useful for researchers who are interested in gathering data to grasp the essence of the human experience.

HERMENEUTIC DESIGN ♦

Some key tenets of the hermeneutic design are (a) interpretation, (b) textual meaning, (c) dialogue, (d) pre-understanding, and (e) tradition. The hermeneutic design deviates from the descriptive nature of which the phenomenological approach is most often associated. This design has a strong focus on reflective interpretation, made evident by Heidegger, who asserted that description is inextricably linked to interpretation. Essentially, this design is based on the fundamental theory that all forms of human awareness are interpretive.

CASE STUDY DESIGN ♦

The case study design is also often used with the phenomenological approach. This design lends itself well to the exploration of meaning of a lived experience of some phenomenon. This design provides the framework for an in-depth analysis of a finite number of participants. Researchers interested in exploring activities of an individual or small group, rather than the shared patterns of group behavior, should follow this design.

WHEN TO USE PHENOMENOLOGY

- Studying people's experiences
- Studying how people make meaning in their lives
- Studying relationships between what happened and how people have come to understand these events
- Exploring how people experience the essence of a particular phenomenon
- Examining the commonalities across individuals

The reader is referred to the following books for further details regarding the phenomenological approach:

Giorgi, A. (2009). *The descriptive phenomenological method in psychology: A modified Huesserlian approach.* Pittsburgh, PA: Duquesne University Press.

Moustakas, C. (1994). *Phenomenological research methods.* Thousand Oaks, CA: Sage.

Smith, J. A., Flowers, P., & Larkin, M. (2009). *Interpretive phenomenological analysis: Theory, method, and research.* Thousand Oaks, CA: Sage.

Example for Figure 14.1

Smith, M. E. (2007). Self-deception among men who are mandated to attend a batterer intervention program. *Perspectives in Psychiatric Care, 43*(4), 193–203.

Research Aim: Gain an understanding of the perceptions of perpetrators of intimate partner violence (IPV) prior to beginning a Batterers' Intervention Program (BIP).

Procedures: Qualitative methods used in this study were conducted according to the existential-phenomenological method outlined by Pollio, Henley, and Thompson (1997). The method of existential phenomenology was used in this study to provide men the opportunity to describe their perceptions concerning the meaning attached to being mandated to attend a BIP.

Figure 14.1 Existential Design

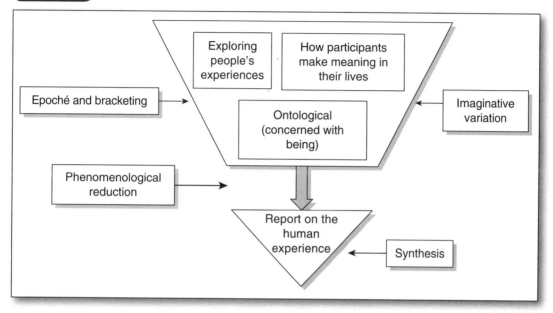

Participants were asked to fill out a demographic questionnaire and then participate in a face-to-face, audiotaped interview. Prior to beginning the study, the first author of Pollio et al. (1997) participated in an individual bracketing interview in order to become more aware of her own biases as a result of her clinical practice with women who experience IPV. Men participated in a face-to-face interview after being mandated to attend a BIP but before attending their first class.

The interviews began with the prompt, "Tell me about your experiences that brought you to a batterer's intervention program." Except for the initial question, all questions flowed from the dialogue. Additional questions were limited to areas of clarification and/or elaboration.

The respondent's own words were used to support a given interpretation. Participant transcripts were then related to each other to identify common patterns or global themes. All of the transcripts were read in a group context to reduce researcher bias. Subsequently, an overall thematic description was developed of the meaning the perpetrator attached to attending a BIP.

Design: Qualitative method utilizing a phenomenological approach with an existential design

Figure 14.2 Transcendental Design

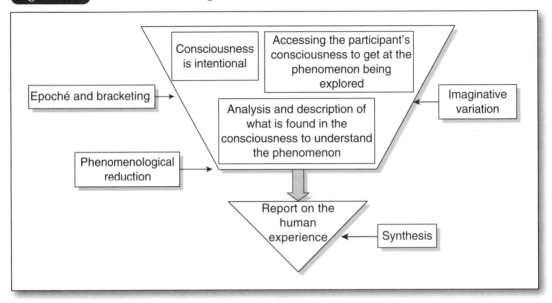

Example for Figure 14.2

Moerer-Urdahl, T., & Creswell, J. W. (2004). Using transcendental phenomenology to explore the "ripple effect" in a leadership mentoring program. *International Journal of Qualitative Methods, 3*(2), 19–35.

Research Aim: To understand the meaning of mentors' experiences with the ripple effect and their experiences of reinvesting in others.

Procedures: Two central questions in this study address key questions that Moustakas (1994) recommended that phenomenologists ask: What were their experiences with the ripple effect? And in what context or situations did they experience it? They were also asked if they considered themselves to be mentors today and, if so, to whom, and if they had been mentored in the past, and by whom.

Detailed telephone interviews were conducted with nine participants, and these interviews were audiotaped, lasting for 25 to 50 minutes. Transcendental phenomenology was chosen as the appropriate methodology for this research as the researchers were searching for an understanding of the meaning of the participants' experiences. Additionally, the systemic procedures and detailed data analysis steps as outlined by Moustakas (1994) are ideal for assisting less experienced researchers. The researchers set aside prejudgments in a process called "epoché," a Greek word meaning to refrain from judgment. The researchers described their own experiences with the phenomenon, identified significant statements in the database from participants, and clustered these statements into meaning units and themes (epoché and bracketing). Next, the researchers synthesized the themes into a description of the experiences of the individuals (textual and structural descriptions) and then constructed a composite description of the meanings and the essences of the experiences.

Design: Qualitative method utilizing a phenomenological approach with a transcendental design.

Figure 14.3 Hermeneutic Design

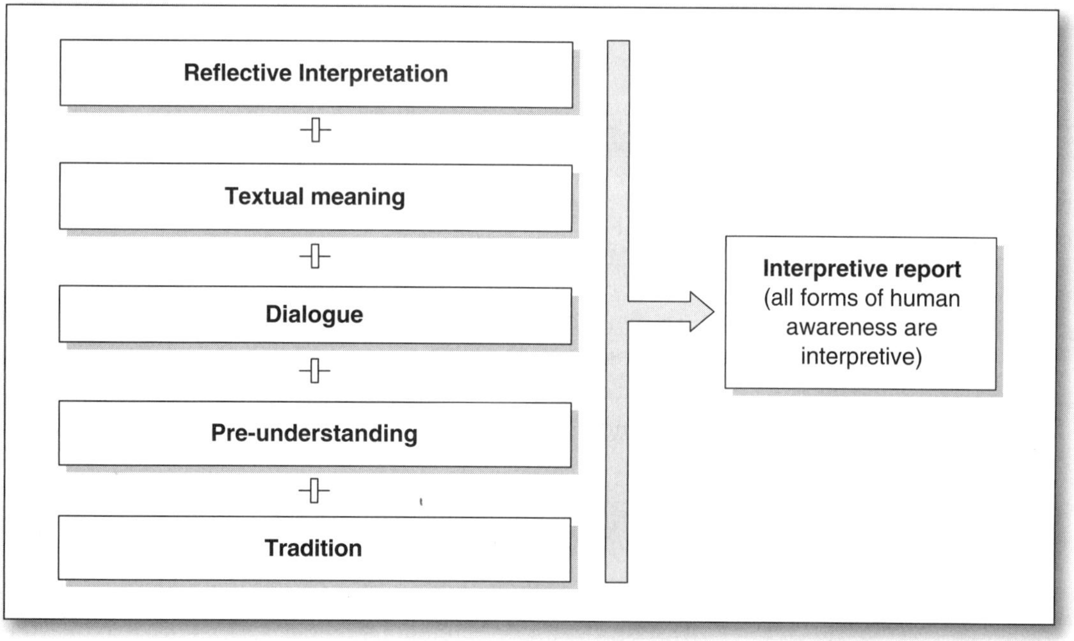

Example for Figure 14.3

Shin, K. R. (2002). Using hermeneutic phenomenology to elicit a sense of body at mid-life. *International Journal of Qualitative Methods, 1*(2), 39–50.

Research Aim: To seek the essence of women's experience of bodily changes caused by menopause and thereby to provide a conceptual framework for women's health promotion education program and theory development

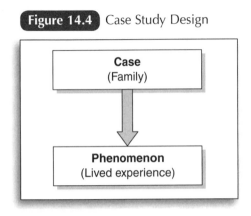

Figure 14.4 Case Study Design

Procedures: This study was a phenomenological and hermeneutic perspective of Korean women who experienced menopause. After exploring the literature, the researcher reflected on artistic depictions of midlife women and conversations with menopausal women in Korea. Phenomenological conversations were conducted with six menopausal women, including two in-depth, tape-recorded interviews and observations. During the initial meeting with participants, the researcher explained the purpose of the study, and then interviewees gave their informed consent to participate in the study. All participants were guaranteed anonymity. Van Manen's (1990) thematic analysis and line-by-line approach, by which every statement of the participants is thoroughly examined, was used to find what their words or sentences implied about their experiences.

Design: Qualitative method utilizing a phenomenological approach with a hermeneutic design

Example for Figure 14.4[1]

Ryndak, D. L., Storch, J. F., & Hoppey, D. (2008). One family's perspective of their experiences with school and district personnel over time related to inclusive educational services for a family member with significant disabilities. *International Journal of Whole Schooling, 4*(2), 29–51.

Research Aim: To understand the impact of placement and special education services, especially in relation to receiving services in inclusive general education classes.

Procedures: The study used a phenomenological lens to explore the experience of one family (mother, father, son, and daughter with significant disabilities) as they sought, lived through, and reflected upon placement and services for the daughter with disabilities. The study focused on how the

---

[1]According to Creswell (2012), this is an example of an intrinsic case study design, which explores a single unusual case. There is also an instrumental case study design that examines a single case to gain insight into a phenomenon and a collective case study that utilizes several cases to provide insight into a phenomenon.

family understood, developed, and socially constructed meanings from the events and interactions that occurred over time as one of the family members moved from receiving special education services and supports in a more restrictive context to receiving special education services and supports in more inclusive contexts.

Phenomenological interviews were conducted three times with each of the daughter's family members (mother, father, and brother). The interviews included open-ended questions to build upon and explore each participant's past and present. Interviews were scheduled two weeks apart for each family member so that the researchers had time to inquire in-depth into the family's lived experiences, while at the same time providing space for the family members to share their own unique insights, stories, and experiences. Thus, each participant was able to reconstruct his or her own experience over time and construct meanings of their own experiences. The researchers then viewed these individual experiences collectively in an attempt to understand the meaning and essence of the family member's collective experiences.

After each interview, the researcher shared the transcript with the interviewee and requested that the family member check the transcript for accuracy, making additions and deletions to further clarify their experiences and perspectives. The researchers used Wolcott's (1994) approach of description, analysis, and interpretation as a method for making sense of interview data. The constant comparison method of reflecting and exploring the data allowed emerging patterns to collectively come into focus.

Design: Qualitative method utilizing a phenomenological approach with a case study design

PART IV

Mixed Methods

T his part includes four popular approaches to mixed methods followed by some of the associated basic designs (accompanied by brief descriptions of published studies that utilize the design). Most of the diagrams of mixed method designs were compiled and adapted from two major sources (Creswell & Plano Clark, 2011; Tashakkori & Teddlie, 2010a). For an in-depth understanding of the application of the design, the full article can be reviewed on the companion website, *A Cross-Section of Research Articles Classified by Design: Quantitative, Qualitative, and Mixed Methods.*

Method		Mixed		
▼		▼		
Research	Experimental	Quasi-Experimental		Nonexperimental
▼		▼		
Approach	Convergence-Parallel	Embedded	Explanatory-Sequential	Exploratory-Sequential
▼		▼		
Design	Parallel-Databases	Data-Transformation	Data-Validation	Multilevel	Embedded-Experiment
	Embedded-Correlational	Embedded Case Study		Follow-Up	Explanations
	Participant-Selection	Theory-Development	Instrument-Development		Treatment-Development

Note: Mixed methods for experimental, quasi-experimental, and nonexperimental research are shown here, followed by the approach and then the design.

Mixed methods examinations combine various aspects of quantitative and qualitative methods (often referred to as quantitative and qualitative strands). Because this type of methodology mixes both the quantitative and qualitative method, the logic of inquiry may include the use of induction, deduction, and abduction. From a philosophical viewpoint, a link has been established between pragmatism and mixed methods. That is, this method was developed as an attempt to legitimatize the use of multiple methodological strategies to answering research questions within a single study, which is considered a more practical approach to research. To conduct a sound mixed method study, it is critical that the researcher has a firm understanding of the distinguishing characteristics of quantitative methods (deduction, confirmation, hypothesis testing, explanation, prediction, standardized data collection, and statistical analysis) and qualitative methods (induction, discovery, exploration, theory generation, *researcher as an instrument* of data collection, and qualitative analysis). The mixed method includes the collection and analyses of quantitative (closed-ended and numerical) and qualitative (open-ended and textual) data (i.e., a quantitative and qualitative research question must be posed, individually analyzed and interpreted, and followed up with an overall interpretation).

Creswell and Plano Clark (2011) noted that one of the primary objectives in designing a mixed method study is to determine if the design should be fixed or emergent. Specifically, a fixed mixed method design is applied when the researcher predetermines the application and integration of a qualitative and quantitative method within a study. On the other hand, an emergent design is conducted when a researcher decides to include a qualitative or quantitative strand within an ongoing examination purely based on necessity. The presentation within this guide falls more toward a typology-based approach. That is, we emphasize the various designs that are classified and developed for the use and application for mixed methods studies. Following those tenets, a researcher must consider many aspects regarding the implementation of a mixed method study. For example, the priority (or emphasis) of the qualitative and quantitative strands should be considered. Equal emphasis can be placed both on the qualitative and quantitative method, or one strand can take priority over the other. The timing of the strands is also relevant. The strands can be implemented concurrently, sequentially, nested (embedded), or multilayered. The mixing of the strands should also be considered, which can happen during the interpretation phase, data collection, data analysis, or at the level of the design.

Philosophically speaking, although mixed methods studies are considered pragmatic, researchers should still be cautious when utilizing the typology-based approach to mixed method research (Collins & O'Cathain, 2009). Many of the "established" mixed methods designs may not fully address the needs of the variety of research scenarios across the various disciplines. Therefore, a more general or generic approach may be warranted. Tashakkori and Teddlie (2010a) produced a sound matrix of the various mixed methods designs, which is summarized in Appendix C. However, most of the designs presented within this part follow Creswell and Plano Clark's (2011) design typology. Within their book, they referred to these designs as variants. In addition, in an earlier version of their text, they referred to these designs as models, many with different names than those seen in their more recent text.

MIXED METHODS LEGEND ♦

The following notations are utilized in the depiction of the various mixed methods approaches and designs:

Design Notation	Design Element
QUAN	Quantitatively driven study
QUAL	Qualitatively driven study
quan	Quantitative data is secondary to qualitative data
qual	Qualitative data is secondary to quantitative data
+	Indicates that quantitative and qualitative data are collected concurrently
→	Indicates that quantitative and qualitative data are collected sequentially
( )	Parentheses indicate that one method is embedded within an emphasized method such as QUAL(quan)
→←	Indicates that the methods are implemented recursively
[ ]	Brackets indicate a mixed method study that is within a series of studies
=	Indicates the transition to mixing methods

Note: The mixed method legend is based on a notation system developed by Morse (1991), Plano Clark (2005), Nastasi et al. (2007), and Morse and Niehaus (2009).

The reader is referred to the following books for further details regarding mixed methods:

Creswell, J. W., & Plano Clark, V. L. (2011). *Designing and conducting mixed methods research* (2nd ed.). Thousand Oaks, CA: Sage.

Morse, J. M., & Niehaus, L. (2009). *Mixed methods design: Principles and procedures*. Walnut Creek, CA: Left Coast Press.

Tashakkori, A., & Teddlie, C. B. (2010a). *SAGE handbook of mixed methods in social & behavioral research* (2nd ed.). Thousand Oaks, CA: Sage.

CHAPTER 15

CONVERGENT-PARALLEL APPROACH

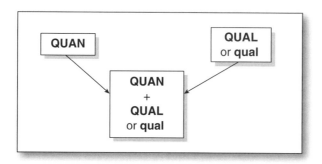

The convergent-parallel approach is a *concurrent* approach and involves the simultaneous collection of qualitative and quantitative data (usually both QUAL and QUAN are the emphasis), followed by the combination and comparisons of these multiple data sources (i.e., the two methods are ultimately merged). This approach involves the collection of different but complementary data on the same phenomena. Thus, it is used for the converging and subsequent interpretation of quantitative and qualitative data. This approach is often referred to as the concurrent triangulation design (single-phase), because the data is collected and analyzed individually but at the same time.

◆ PARALLEL-DATABASES DESIGN

The parallel-databases design is structured so the QUAN and QUAL data are collected separately (not within the same measures) but at the same time (concurrently). The analyses of data are also analyzed concurrently. The results are then converged by comparing and contrasting the data en route to one overall interpretive framework. This design allows researchers to validate data by converging the QUAN results with the QUAL findings. This design is also referred to as a triangulation design and convergence model as seen in Seifert, Goodman, King, and Baxter Magolda's (2010) examination.

◆ DATA-TRANSFORMATION DESIGN

The data-transformation design allows the researcher to collect QUAN and QUAL data separately but concurrently. Following the subsequent analyses, data are transformed by either transforming QUAN to QUAL *or* QUAL to QUAN. Therefore, the data are mixed during this stage, followed by the subsequent analyses.

◆ DATA-VALIDATION DESIGN

The validating quantitative data design is used to validate QUAN data with qual findings. Data from QUAN and qual are collected together (within the same measures), not separately. Within this design, the qual findings are not the emphasis, therefore they are not subject to rigorous data reduction or analysis.

◆ MULTILEVEL DESIGN

The multilevel design was originally introduced by Tashakkori and Teddlie (2002). This design allows the researcher to utilize different methodological techniques for addressing QUAN and QUAL data within a system. The QUAN results and QUAL findings from each level are then merged to provide an overall interpretation.

Figure 15.1 Parallel-Databases Design

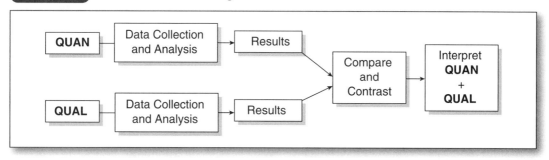

Note: Any research design designated as experimental, quasi-experimental, or nonexperimental research can be used for the QUAN phase, and any approach designated under the qualitative method can be used for the QUAL phase.

Example for Figure 15.1

Hall-Kenyon, K. M., Bingham, G. E., & Korth, B. B. (2009). How do linguistically diverse students fare in full- and half-day kindergarten? Examining academic achievement, instructional quality, and attendance. *Early Education and Development, 20,* 25–52.

Research Questions

> *Quantitative:* What are the effects of instructional quality on academic achievement (math and literacy)?

> *Qualitative:* What are teacher and administrator perceptions of full- and half-day programs, and how do teachers' instructional behaviors influence academic achievement?

> *Mixed Method:* To what extent do the QUAN data and QUAL data converge?

Procedures

> *Quantitative:* Eight kindergarten classrooms were used: four full-day classrooms and four half-day classrooms. The four kindergarten classrooms from the treatment school were in the first year of implementing a full-day pilot program. The four classrooms were receiving a half-day program as usual. Students' academic achievement was assessed prior to and at the end of the school year utilizing the following measures: (a) Peabody Picture Vocabulary Test, (b) Phonological

Awareness Literacy Screening, and (c) the Applied Problems subtest of the Wood-Cock Johnson III.

Qualitative: To assess the instructional quality of the teaching programs, the Classroom Assessment Scoring System was used, which includes observing teachers' instructional behaviors. Additionally, teachers and administrators from both schools were interviewed at the end of the school year using a structured interview protocol. Interview transcriptions were analyzed inductively by two of the three authors. The two authors independently read all of the interview transcriptions and coded each separate idea generated by the teachers and administrators into categories.

Design: A mixed methods study utilizing nonexperimental research with a convergent-parallel approach and a parallel-databases design.[1]

Figure 15.2   Data-Transformation Design

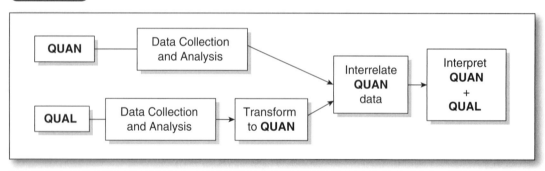

Note: Any research design designated as experimental, quasi-experimental, or nonexperimental research can be used for the QUAN phase, and any approach designated under the qualitative method can be used for the QUAL phase.

Example for Figure 15.2

Kaldjian, L. C., Jones, E. W., Rosenthal, G. E., Tripp-Reimer, T., & Hillis, S. L. (2006). An empirically derived taxonomy of factors affecting physicians' willingness to disclose medical errors. *Journal of General Internal Medicine, 21,* 942–948.

---

[1]The authors refer to the design as a concurrent triangulation strategy, which follows the parallel-databases design.

Research Questions

> *Quantitative and Qualitative:* What is the taxonomy of factors that affect voluntary disclosure of errors by physicians?

> *Mixed Method:* To what extent do the same types of data (QUAN and QUAL) confirm each other?

Procedures: Initially, a literature review was conducted. Articles were selected that addressed the experience of selected physicians. Specific factors were identified and selected from the review process. Labels for facilitating and impeding factors were derived through an iterative process. The iterative process of naming served to synthesize the linguistic heterogeneity of the literature reviewed. Next, focus groups were conducted to discuss factors related to physician self-disclosure of medical errors to institutions, patients, and colleagues. The factors identified from the focus groups were combined with the factors from the literature review. The next step included a pile-sorting task. The pile-sorting results were entered into a database for hierarchical cluster analysis to construct clustering schemes. For each pair of factors, a "distance" score was computed. Four types of hierarchical cluster analysis were performed. Focus groups were then used to validate the clustering scheme. The resulting taxonomy was independently reviewed by two qualified individuals in ethics.

Design: A mixed methods study utilizing nonexperimental research with a convergent-parallel approach and a data-transformation design

Example for Figure 15.3

Abrams, L. S., Shannon, S. K. S., & Sangalang, C. (2008). Transition services for incarcerated youth: A mixed methods evaluation study. *Children and Youth Services Review, 30,* 522–535.

Research Aims: Examine recidivism outcomes for youth participants in a transitional living program at 1-year postrelease; explore child protective services involvement as a risk factor for recidivism at 1-year postrelease; compare youth and staff perspectives on the strengths and limitations of the transitional living program in preparing youth for community reentry.

Research Question (Mixed Method): To what extent do the open-ended themes support the survey results?

Figure 15.3 Data-Validation Design

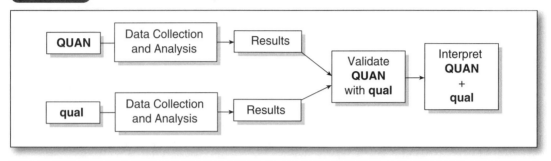

Note: Any research design designated as experimental, quasi-experimental, or nonexperimental research can be used for the QUAN phase, and cross sections of qualitative data can be collected for the qual phase.

Procedures

Quantitative: Archival data were retrieved from the state administrative data system for juvenile and adult offenders and official client case records. Variables retrieved from the state administrative data included basic demographic information, number of prior arrests, new substantiated crimes up to 1-year postrelease, and participation in the transition living program. Variables retrieved from the intake forms included a history of child welfare system involvement, family structure, substance abuse, and additional comprehensive descriptors of each case. The primary independent variable was participation in the 6-week transition living program. Child welfare system involvement was another independent variable. The dependent variable for the analysis was recidivism at 1-year postrelease. Control variables retrieved from the administrative database included number of prior arrests, race, and age at admission to program.

Qualitative: The sample for the qualitative component of the study included 10 youth who participated in the transition living program and were interviewed repeatedly over a 6-month period. Interviews with youth were semistructured. The interviews were taped with a digital recording device. Interviews with staff occurred after the youth-interview component of the project was completed. Questions were geared to gather staff perspectives on the important components of transition, the benefits and limitations of the transition program, and their views on the challenges of youths' postrelease environments. Digitally taped interviews were transcribed verbatim and further reduced via data analysis.

Figure 15.4 Multilevel Design

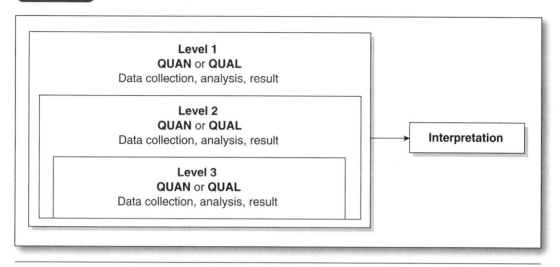

Note: Any research design designated as experimental, quasi-experimental, or nonexperimental research can be used for the QUAN phases, and any approach designated under the qualitative method can be used for the QUAL phases.

Design: A mixed methods study utilizing nonexperimental research with a convergent-parallel approach and a data-validation design

Example for Figure 15.4

Elliott, M. S., & Williams, D. I. (2002). A qualitative evaluation of an employee counselling service from the perspective of client, counselor, and organization. *Counselling Psychology Quarterly, 15*(2), 201–208.

Research Questions

> *Quantitative and Qualitative:* What is the degree of congruence across the aims and expectations of all three parties (the client, counselor, and organization)? Are their needs being met?

> *Mixed Method:* What similarities and differences exist across levels of analyses?

Procedures: Data were collected from three different levels: (a) the client, (b) the counselor, and (c) the organization. Client data included semistructured interviews with each party. The form of the interviews followed the client's path from before counseling to the present. Participants were interviewed between 6 and 20 months posttermination of counseling. The counselor completed an "encounter questionnaire" with respect to each of the clients interviewed in the study. The counselor was asked for an evaluative trace through counseling for each client concentrating on relevant areas such as conceptualization, process and outcome, impact on the organization, and professional and personal issues raised by the work. An intense in-depth study of the counselor perspective was conducted through a series of four linked interviews with one of the counselors. Organizational data were also collected from semistructured interviews with high-level officials within the organization. Awareness was assessed by administering questionnaires to a stratified sample of the staff. Bottom-line benefits were assessed by reviewing the sickness records of the client group.

Design: A mixed methods study utilizing nonexperimental research with a convergent parallel approach and a multilevel design

CHAPTER 16

EMBEDDED APPROACH

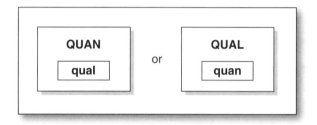

T he embedded approach is a *nested* approach and is used when one type of data (QUAN or QUAL) is most critical to the researcher. This approach is used when different questions require different types of data (qualitative and quantitative). The embedded approach is used when one type of data clearly plays a secondary role and would not be meaningful if not embedded within the primary data set. The embedded approach is also useful when the researcher logistically cannot place equal priority on both types of data or simply has little experience with one of the forms of data. Many variants of the embedded approach have been proposed, such as the embedded narrative and ethnography designs. For many years, clinical psychology has utilized a form of the embedded narrative case study design (see Kazdin, 2002). That is, a clinician would collect relevant quantitative indices and qualitative data and develop a cohesive narrative account explaining the clinical features of the individual case. Based on theoretical and logistical considerations, many other design variants of the embedded approach can be meshed with many of the traditional designs presented in this book. These are sometimes referred to as hybrid designs.

♦ EMBEDDED-EXPERIMENT DESIGN

The embedded-experiment design allows the researcher to embed qual data within experimental research. If the research is considered quasi-experimental, then the design can be referred to as an embedded quasi-experimental design. The researcher can use any research design that is designated as such (i.e., within- or between-subject approaches). This model can be further designated as one-phase, which allows the researcher to collect the qual data during the intervention, or two-phase, where the researcher collects qual data before and after the experimental or quasi-experimental phase.

♦ EMBEDDED-CORRELATIONAL DESIGN

The embedded-correlational design allows the researcher to embed qual data within nonexperimental research (observational approach). The designs can be either predictive or explanatory. QUAN data is the emphasis within this design.

♦ EMBEDDED CASE STUDY DESIGN

The embedded case study design can be applied as a means to explore a phenomenon within its real-world context when the boundaries between phenomena and context are not clearly evident in which multiple data sources and types (QUAL and quan) are used. QUAL data is the emphasis while the quan data provides a supplementary role to the qualitative findings. An ethnographic or narrative approach is commonly applied to guide the tenets of the case study design.

Example for Figure 16.1[1]

Zydney, J. M. (2008). Cognitive tools for scaffolding students defining an ill-structured problem. *Journal of Educational Computing Research, 38*(4), 353–385.

---

[1]The example uses the one-phase approach to the embedded design (also known as a concurrent nested mixed methods design) with the qualitative data collected during the intervention. A two-phase approach can also be used when the qualitative data is collected before or after the intervention.

Figure 16.1 Embedded-Experiment Design (One-Phase)

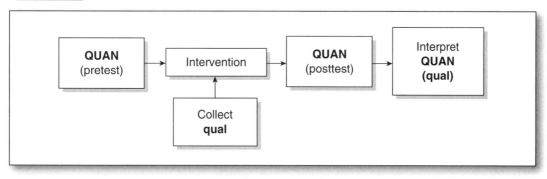

Note: Any research design designated as a between-subjects or repeated-measures approach can be used for the QUAN phase, and a cross section of qualitative data can be collected for the qual phase.

Research Questions

> *Quantitative and Qualitative:* What is the effect of cognitive tools in scaffolding students defining an ill-structured problem, as measured by (a) students' problem understanding, (b) ability to generate questions, and (c) ability to formulate hypotheses on how to solve the problem?

> *Mixed Method:* How do the qual results inform the development of the treatment? What additional information is obtained during the trial from the qual data? How do the qual results expand on the QUAN data?

Procedures: During the first session, students were introduced to the project and completed the fluency test. During the second session, students met their supervisor and their client, who explained the acid rain problem faced by the company. During the third session, students discussed what information they needed and saw a brief demonstration on how to find information within the *Pollution Solution* learning environment. During the fourth session, students independently researched and took notes about the problem. The students with the higher order thinking tool and the combination tool completed their status reports, and students in the organization tool and control groups continued their research. After completing their research plans, the students completed a questioning assessment. After this assessment, the students answered a few survey questions to determine if they were absent at any time, worked at home, lost any data during the study, or discussed their work outside of class.

The quantitative and qualitative data were collected concurrently (when data are collected during the intervention, it is considered a one-phase approach). The quantitative data were obtained through computer-based assessments, and the qualitative data were captured through classroom observations. The classes were randomly assigned to one of four conditions of the treatment. The control group provided students with directions to write the research plan. Another group received the organization tool. Field notes carefully described the classroom activity during the study, and special notes were made of any differences between the classes. To analyze these field notes, qualitative differences among the classes were coded. These qualitative differences were organized in a chart along with the quantitative findings in order to see whether the statistical differences could be explained by the qualitative differences among the classes.

Design: A mixed methods study utilizing experimental research with an embedded approach and an embedded-experiment design

Figure 16.2 Embedded-Correlational Design

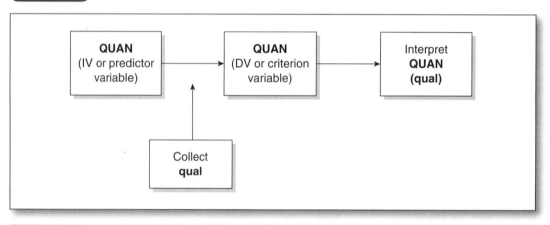

Note: The observational design can be either explanatory or predictive.

Example for Figure 16.2

Forchuk, C., Norman, R., Malla, A., Martin, M., McLean, T., & Cheng, S., . . . Gibney, C. (2002). Schizophrenia and the motivation for smoking. *Perspectives in Psychiatric Care, 38*(2), 41–49.

Research Questions

> *Quantitative and Qualitative:* Are individuals with schizophrenia motivated to smoke for relief of psychiatric symptoms and to relieve antipsychotic medication side effects?

Mixed Method: How does the qual data add to the expansion of the constructs in the correlational model?

Procedures: Participants were selected randomly by staff members at various settings. After informed consent was obtained, the interviewer and participant agreed on a meeting place. The interview took approximately 1 hour. All data were collected through an interview format, which included the questionnaires and open-ended questions.

Data were collected through a single interview with individuals who have been diagnosed with schizophrenia for a minimum of 1 year and who smoke. The research design included two components to examine smoking and schizophrenia: (a) a descriptive, correlational design that described and examined the relationships among psychiatric symptoms, medication side effects, and reasons for smoking; and (b) a content analysis of open-ended questions related to the subjective experience of smoking.

Design: A mixed methods study utilizing nonexperimental research with an embedded approach and an embedded-correlational design

Figure 16.3 Embedded Case Study Design

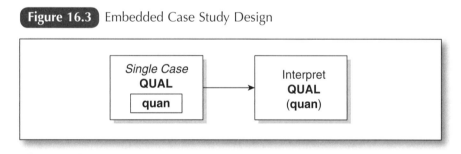

Note: Yin (2009) refers to the term "embedded" as collecting data from multiple sources regardless of method. The term "embedded" in this example refers to the collection of quan data within the QUAL data-collection procedures.

Example for Figure 16.3

Beeke, S., Wilkinson, R., & Maxin, J. (2007). Individual variation in agrammatism: A single case study of the influence of interaction. *Journal of Language and Communication Disorders, 42*(6), 629–647.

Research Questions

Quantitative and Qualitative: (1) In what ways do grammatical structure, verbs, and argument structure qualitatively reveal the single case?; and (2) What is the influence of the interaction on the structure of the utterances from the case?

Mixed Method: How does the quan data add to and expand on the QUAL findings?

Procedures: A single case diagnosed with severe and chronic agrammatism is videotaped completing a set of spoken tests. Videos were also taken of independent conversations between the case and family members. The case was administered six different measures, which were qualitatively driven but contain quantitative components. These include the Psycholinguistic Assessment of Language Processing in Aphasia, Subtest 53: Spoken Picture Naming (PALPA), Thematic Roles in Production (TRIP), Verb and Sentence Test (VAST), Cookie Theft Picture Description, Dinner Party Cartoon Strip Description, and the Cinderella Story-Telling technique. The PALPA, TRIP, and VAST were analyzed and assigned quantitative values based on the outcome data. The data from the remaining assessments were microanalyzed based on all the utterances in each set. The data were then combined and discussed as a whole utilizing a narrative approach.

Design: A mixed methods study utilizing nonexperimental research with an embedded approach and an embedded case study design

CHAPTER **17**

EXPLANATORY-SEQUENTIAL APPROACH

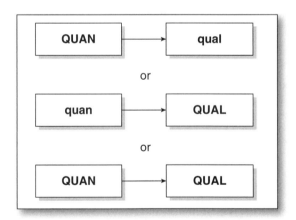

T he explanatory-sequential approach is a *sequential* approach and is used when the researcher is interested in following up the quantitative results with qualitative data. Thus, the qualitative data is used in the subsequent interpretation and clarification of the results from the quantitative data analysis. In many instances, because the QUAN design is the emphasis, a generic qual design is utilized in explanatory approaches. This two-phase approach is particularly useful for a researcher interested in explaining the findings from the first phase of the study with the qualitative data collected during phase 2. However, either the

163

qualitative or quantitative data (or both equally) may be the primary focus of the study (see figure above). For example, the qualitative phase is often emphasized when using the participant-selection design.

◆ FOLLOW-UP EXPLANATIONS DESIGN

The follow-up explanations design provides a framework for the researcher to collect qual data in order to expand on the QUAN data and results. Within this design, a researcher analyzes the relevant QUAN results and then uses the qual findings to further explain the initial QUAN results. Thus, the primary emphasis is on the QUAN results.

◆ PARTICIPANT-SELECTION DESIGN

The participant-selection design involves a two-phase process: First, the participant selection (phase 1) is conducted using a quantitative method, followed by a qualitative data collection phase (phase 2). Participants are selected during the first phase based on parameters set a priori by the researcher as a means of purposeful sampling. Thus, the quan phase is strictly used to generate the sample.

Figure 17.1 Follow-Up Explanation Design

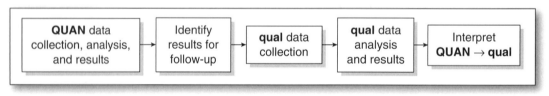

Note: Any research design designated as experimental, quasi-experimental, or nonexperimental research can be used for the initial QUAN phase of this design, and cross sections of qualitative data can be collected for the qual phase.

Example for Figure 17.1

Lee, K. S., Osborne, R. E., Hayes, K. A., & Simoes, R. A. (2008). The effects of pacing on the academic testing performance of college students with ADHD: A mixed methods study. *Journal of Educational Computing Research, 39*(2), 123–141.

Research Questions

Quantitative and Qualitative: What is the relationship between computer-paced and student-paced item presentation on the academic test performance in college students diagnosed with attention-deficit/ hyperactivity disorder (ADHD)?

Mixed Method: In what ways do the qual data help to explain the QUAN results?

Procedures: Participants were randomly assigned to one of two treatment conditions. In the computer-paced testing condition, the students were allowed 90 seconds per question and were forced to move on to the next question when the time expired. In the student-paced testing condition, students were allowed an average of 90 seconds per question but were not forced to move on to the next question. Upon completion of either the computer-paced or student-paced test, each participant was individually interviewed face to face by the primary investigator to explore the student's perception of the testing experience.

This exploratory study utilized a follow-up explanation with quasi-experimental design (QUAN) to explore and explain the effects of paced item presentation for college students diagnosed with ADHD. The goal was to analyze two testing conditions and interpret their impact on a small number of participants who participated in the study.

Design: A mixed methods study utilizing quasi-experimental research with an explanatory-sequential approach and a follow-up explanations design

Example for Figure 17.2

Hannan, M., Happ, M. B., & Charron-Prochownik, D. (2009). Mothers' perspectives about reproductive health discussion with adolescent daughters with diabetes. *The Diabetes Educator, 35*(2), 265–273.

Research Aim and Question

Quantitative and Qualitative: Explore mothers' perspectives about reproductive health (RH) discussions with their adolescent daughters with diabetes.

Mixed Method: Which cases provide the best insights into the quan results?

Figure 17.2 Participant-Selection Design

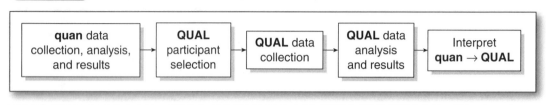

Note: Cross sections of quantitative data can be collected for the initial quan phase, and any approach and design designated under the qualitative method can be used for the QUAL phase.

Procedures: The researchers followed a two-phase sequential explanatory process. Phase 1 involved the selection of participants from a larger study sample through purposeful sampling. More specifically, criterion-related purposeful sampling was used to select a subset of 10 mothers from the total sample. Participants were selected for variation on the following parameters: baseline knowledge (modified Family Planning Behavior and Diabetes Study questionnaire) and intention scores (modified Initiating Discussion questionnaire), daughters' group assignment (IG or CG), and daughters' age group. Data from questionnaires administered in phase 1 were used for criterion-related sampling.

Phase 2, the focus of the report, was a qualitative descriptive study using open-ended semistructured telephone interviews. The principal investigator conducted interviews via the telephone using a semistructured interview guide that began with a grand tour question ("I'd like for you to tell me about discussing RH issues, such as monthly periods, sex, birth control, or pregnancy, with your daughter"). Additional questions probed the mother's perceptions of who initiated discussions, timing of discussions, barriers and facilitators to discussions, and her comfort with initiation of discussion. There was no time limit to the interviews, which generally lasted 20 to 30 minutes. Interviews were digitally recorded, transferred to a secure laptop, transcribed verbatim, and reviewed for accuracy. The interviews were conducted over a 1-year period of time, which began 2 years after mothers' completion of the quantitative portion of this study. Qualitative content analysis techniques were used to analyze the interview transcripts.

Design: A mixed methods study utilizing nonexperimental research with an explanatory-sequential approach and a participant-selection design.

CHAPTER **18**

EXPLORATORY-SEQUENTIAL APPROACH

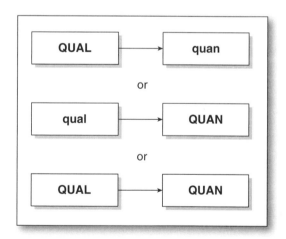

T he exploratory-sequential approach is a *sequential* approach and is used when the researcher is interested in following up qualitative findings with quantitative analysis. This two-phase approach is particularly useful for a researcher interested in developing a new instrument, taxonomy, or treatment protocol (Creswell & Plano Clark, 2011). The researcher uses the qualitative (exploratory) findings from the first phase to help develop the instrument or treatment and then tests this product during the second phase (quantitative). In general, when variables are unknown, this approach is useful to identify important variables (phase 1) for subsequent quantitative analysis (phase 2). It is also a useful approach for revising existing instruments and treatment protocols as well as for developing and testing a theory. Although the QUAL phase is usually the primary focus, either the qualitative or quantitative phase (or both equally) may be the primary emphasis of the study (see figure shown earlier).

◆ INSTRUMENT-DEVELOPMENT DESIGN

The instrument-development design is often QUAN emphasized and provides a framework for the researcher to first develop and then test (psychometrically) an instrument on a specific population. With this design, the researcher utilizes the qualitative results to help construct the instrument and validates the instrument during the subsequent quantitative phase. Either the qualitative or quantitative data (or both equally) may be the primary emphasis of the study.

◆ THEORY-DEVELOPMENT DESIGN

The theory-development (and taxonomy-development) design is often QUAL emphasized. The researcher uses the qualitative data collected during the first phase to identify, develop, and construct a classification system or theory. The taxonomy or theory is subsequently analyzed quantitatively during phase 2. Oftentimes, researchers will use the qualitative findings to develop their research questions, which guide the quantitative phase of the study. Either the qualitative or quantitative data (or both equally) may be the primary emphasis of the study.

◆ TREATMENT-DEVELOPMENT DESIGN

The treatment-development design is both QUAL and QUAN emphasized and provides a framework for the researcher to develop and then test a treatment protocol or approach with a specific population. With this design, the researcher utilizes the qualitative results to help construct the treatment protocol and then tests the efficacy of the treatment during the subsequent quantitative phase. Either the qualitative or quantitative data (or both equally) may be the primary emphasis of the study.

Figure 18.1 Instrument-Development Design

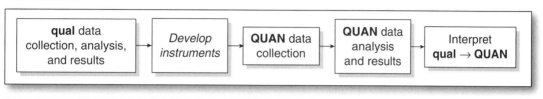

Note: Cross sections of qualitative data can be collected for the qual phase, and an explanatory design within the observational approach is typically used for the QUAN phase of this design.

Example for Figure 18.1

Zolotor, A. J., Runyan, D. K., Dunne, M. P., Jain, D., Petrus, H. R., Ramirez, C., . . . Isaeva, O. (2009). ISPCAN Child Abuse Screening Tool Children's Version (ICAST-C): Instrument development and multi-national pilot testing. *Child Abuse & Neglect, 33*(11), 833–841.

Research Aims and Question

> *Phase 1:* Develop a child victimization survey.
>
> *Phase 2:* Examine the performance of the instrument through a set of international pilot studies.

Mixed Method: What items and scales represent the qual findings?

Procedures: The researchers developed the initial draft of the instrument after receiving input from scientists and practitioners representing 40 countries. The original instrument contained 82 screener questions as to the potentially victimizing experiences at home and school or work. Volunteers from the larger group of scientists participating in the Delphi review of the ISPCAN Child Abuse Screen Tool–Parent Version (ICAST-P) and Retrospective Version (ICAST-R) reviewed the Children's Version (ICAST-C) by e-mail in two rounds, resulting in a final instrument. The ICAST-C was then translated and back-translated into six languages and field tested in four countries using a convenience sample of 571 children 12–17 years of age, selected from schools and classrooms to which the investigators had easy access.

Design: A mixed methods study utilizing nonexperimental research with an exploratory-sequential approach and an instrument-development design

Figure 18.2 Theory-Development Design

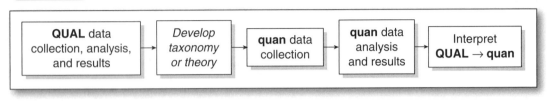

Note: Any approach and design designated under the qualitative method can be used for the QUAL phase, and cross sections of quantitative data can be collected for the quan phase.

Example for Figure 18.2

Kartalova-O'Doherty, Y., & Doherty, D. T. (2008). Coping strategies and styles of family carers of persons with enduring mental illness: A mixed methods analysis. *Scandinavian Journal of Caring Sciences, 22*(1), 19–28.

Research Aims and Question

> *Phase 1:* Identify and describe the coping strategies and styles of participants.

> *Phase 2:* Investigate the interaction of identified coping strategies and styles with the sociodemographic characteristics of participants and then explore the interaction of the identified coping styles with contextual factors.

Mixed Method: How do the quan results generalize to the QUAL findings?

Procedures: During phase 1, content analysis was used to explore and classify the self-reported coping strategies and styles of participants as emerging from the original interviews. Statistical procedures were employed during phase 2 to explore the interaction of coping styles with contextual factors, including duration of illness, living arrangements, and occupational status of the ill relative. The mixed methods analysis allowed the researchers to explore the qualitative data from the perspective of well-established quantitative findings in the areas of stress and coping and to further interpret the emergent findings using qualitative data.

Design: A mixed methods study utilizing nonexperimental research with an exploratory-sequential approach and a theory-development design

Figure 18.3 Treatment-Development Design

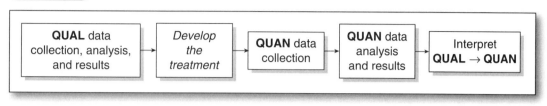

Note: Any approach and design designated under the qualitative method can be used for the QUAL phase, and any research design designated as experimental, quasi-experimental, or nonexperimental research can be used for the initial QUAN phase of this design.

Example for Figure 18.3

Nagel, T., Robinson, G., Condon, J., & Trauer, T. (2009). Approach to treatment of mental illness and substance dependence in remote indigenous communities: Results of a mixed methods study. *Australian Journal of Rural Health, 17*(4), 174–182.

Research Aims and Question

> *Phase 1:* Develop a culturally adapted brief intervention for indigenous people with chronic mental illness.

> *Phase 2:* Evaluate the efficacy of the brief intervention.

Mixed Method: What treatment was developed from the QUAL findings?

Procedures: An exploratory phase of qualitative research was followed by a nested randomized controlled trial. The first phase of the study focused on understanding local perspectives of mental health through collaboration with local aboriginal mental health workers (AMHWs). These perspectives were then incorporated into a brief motivational care planning (MCP) intervention. Qualitative data providing rich description of the personal experiences of patients were gathered concurrently with the randomized controlled trial and integrated into the final analysis.

The exploratory phase (phase 1) of the study was conducted over 12 months. Data were collected during 15 field trips of 1- to 3-day duration. Group and individual interviews were supplemented by informal observation.

Three key themes emerged: the importance of family, the strength gained from traditional and cultural activities, and the importance of a storytelling approach to sharing information.

During phase 2, 49 indigenous patients with mental illness and 37 carers were recruited. Patient participants were randomly allocated to two groups using a block randomization random number sequence technique after completion of baseline measures. Participants, carers, and AMHWs were given an explanation of the project in spoken, written, and pictorial format. Where necessary, translation to local language was provided by the AMHWs in order to ensure that informed consent was obtained. The treatment was delivered at baseline in the first group (the "early treatment" group) and at 6 months in the second group (the "late treatment" group).

Design: A mixed methods study utilizing both nonexperimental and experimental research with an exploratory-sequential approach and a treatment-development design

CHAPTER 19

MIXED METHODS, CASE STUDIES, AND SINGLE-CASE APPROACHES

As previously noted, the primary reason for utilizing mixed methods is to maximize the use of blending methods to answer research questions within a study (i.e., converge and confirm results from different methodological techniques). Keep in mind that the use and application of mixed methods in education and the social and behavioral sciences are still relatively new and evolving (see Tashakkori & Teddlie, 2010b). Many of the designs presented are difficult to locate in the literature. That is, authors typically do not indicate the name of the mixed method research design (or use different names) in their published manuscripts. Nonetheless, there is a growing interest and need for the application of mixed methods as a means to reveal complex and relevant scientific inquiries. There are many applications of mixed methods not yet identified in the literature or in textbooks that should be proposed. Based on our observations in the field, we recommend combining qualitative methodology with the family of A-B designs (i.e., the single-case approach). Developing a structure and framework for mixed method single-case approaches can strengthen the results from $N = 1$ designs en route to implying causal relations.

The mixed method single-case approach still maintains the key characteristics (as defined by the quantitative methodological tenets), which are (a) continuous assessment (repeated measures), (b) baseline assessment, (c) accounting for stability in performance, and (d) the introduction of varied phases. However, the qualitative (qual) method should serve as a secondary role to the quantitative (QUAN) method (i.e., the emphasis is on the design of the single-case approach). Because the qualitative method is secondary, a sound generic qualitative design should usually suffice for these applications. For example, a cross section of qual data can be collected concurrently, sequentially, or can be nested (embedded) within the design. When applying these designs, and staying true to the tenets of mixed methodology, it is critical to discuss how the qual findings add to, explain, and expand on the QUAN results.

◆ MIXED-METHOD A-B-A DESIGNS

Although we present diagrams of the A-B-A mixed method design, it should be noted that any version of the A-B family of designs can be utilized (e.g., A-B-A-B, A-B-C, multiple baseline, changing criterion, etc.). Diagram 19.1 is the A-B-A concurrent design. The qual data is collected concurrently (simultaneously) throughout the process of the design. Next, Diagram 19.2 illustrates the A-B-A sequential design. Within this design, qual data is collected sequentially throughout the various phases of the treatment and baseline applications. In addition to collecting qual data between each session, the qual data can also be collected prior to and after the baseline and follow-up sessions. Last, Diagram 19.3 is an A-B-A nested design. This design allows the researcher to collect qual data prior to and following the application of the entire design. See the diagrams for diagrammatic representations of the mixed methods single-case approaches. The applications of these designs should always be based on theoretical and logistical considerations.

Sequential Case Study Single-Case Design

As seen in Diagram 19.1, we propose the application of combining the case study design and the single-case approach as a means to provide a truly in-depth and rigorous analysis and assessment of a single participant ($N = 1$). This design would be considered an exploratory approach, and the emphasis would be both on qualitative (QUAL) and quantitative (QUAN) methods sequentially delivered. This design is applicable in a wide array of disciplines,

Diagram 19.1 A-B-A Concurrent Design

Case	Method	Baseline A	Treatment B	Baseline A
1	QUAN	O_n	O_n	O_n
	qual	O_{qual}	O_{qual}	O_{qual}

Time ▶

Note: Multiple forms and types of qual data can be collected during each phase.

Diagram 19.2 A-B-A Sequential Design

Case	Baseline A		Treatment B		Baseline A	
1	O_n	O_{qual}	O_n	O_{qual}	O_n	O_{qual}

Time ▶

Note: A cross section of qual data can be collected at any point between treatment and baseline phases.

Diagram 19.3 A-B-A Nested Design

Case	Pretest	Baseline A	Treatment B	Baseline A	Posttest
1	O_{qual}	O_n	O_n	O_n	O_{qual}

Time ▶

Note: A cross section of qual data is collected prior to and following the completion of the study.

such as education, psychiatry, rehabilitation, and medicine. The general steps would include, for example, utilizing the case study approach to detail and reveal the intricate cognitive and behavioral patterns associated with a child diagnosed with a pervasive developmental disorder. Information gathered from the case study can then be applied to one or more types of cognitive behavioral therapies implemented and the effects assessed through the use of an A-B-A design. As with all mixed methods studies, the results from the case study and A-B-A design should be analyzed and discussed individually and collectively.

Figure 19.1 Sequential Case Study Single-Case Design

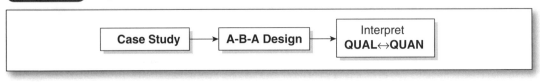

Note: Any version of the case study (see Appendix B) can be used as defined by Yin (2009) or Creswell (2012), and any version of the A-B family of designs can be utilized.

CHAPTER 20

CONCLUSION

The primary objective of this reference guide is to help researchers understand and select appropriate designs for their investigations within the field, lab, or virtual environment. Lacking a proper conceptualization of a research design makes it difficult to apply an appropriate design based on the research question(s) or stated hypotheses. Implementing a flawed or inappropriate design will unequivocally lead to spurious, meaningless, or invalid results. Again, the concept of validity cannot be emphasized enough when conducting research. Validity maintains many facets (e.g., statistical validity or validity pertaining to psychometric properties of instrumentation), operates on a continuum, and deserves equal attention at each level of the research process. Nonetheless, the research question, hypothesis, objective, or aim is the primary step for the selection of a research design.

RESEARCH QUESTIONS ♦

Simply put, the primary research question sets the foundation and decision of the application of the most appropriate research design. However, there are several terms related to research questions that should be distinguished. First, in general, studies will include a research topic, a problem statement, and a purpose statement. The topic is a general statement regarding the area of interest and the problem statement indentifies the area of need or concern. Although many published articles and dissertations do not specifically clarify and indicate a topic, a problem statement, and a purpose statement, the fact is that these elements still implicitly exist within the study. Based on the variables located in a strong problem statement, the literature review and establishment of the theoretical framework is developed. The purpose statement is then used to clarify the focus of the study, and finally the primary research question ensues. Research studies can also include hypotheses or research objectives. Many qualitative studies include research aims as opposed to research questions. In quantitative methods (this includes mixed methods), the research question (hypotheses and objectives) determines (a) the population (and sample) to be investigated, (b) the context, (c) the data to be collected, and (d) the research design to be employed. For example, if the primary question is descriptive, then the research will be non-experimental and a survey approach should be employed. If the primary question is comparative, then any approach and design that falls under the category of quasi-experimental or experimental research should be used. If the primary question is relational, then an observational approach and a predictive or explanatory design should be applied. It should be noted that these are only general guidelines and the application of the appropriate design relative to the primary research can vary depending on the specific research scenario and the field from which the examination is to be applied. The reader is referred to White (2009) for an in-depth review of the development of research questions for social scientists.

◆ EVALUATION APPROACHES

Within this book, we cover some of the most common research designs in quantitative, qualitative, and mixed methods. However, we have not included evaluation approaches or program evaluation models. Evaluation approaches are primarily used to judge (or evaluate) the merit or worth of a program, product, or process. Although many evaluation approaches have emerged from the traditional framework of social sciences' research, there is a point where evaluation and research diverge in several key areas. More specifically, the primary goal of research (quasi-experimental or experimental and non-experimental) is to (a) expand, confirm, or develop theories; (b) seek outcomes; (c) generalize the findings (to the subject or population of interest in quantitative methods); and (d) disseminate the results. Alternatively, the primary goal of an evaluation is to draw judgments based on the findings; however, instead of disseminating the findings, the results are fed back to the stakeholders and ultimately integrated into the program of interest. Another key distinction between research and evaluation is that a researcher develops the research objectives or questions, whereas the stakeholders typically develop the aims or objectives for the evaluator to pursue.

Despite these differences, there are many instances where research and evaluation do overlap (i.e., converge). Based on the objectives set forth by the stakeholders and considering the type of program evaluation model to be employed, the appropriate research design should be embedded within the evaluation approach. Specifically, the process of selecting a research design within a program evaluation can take place once the research questions or objectives have been determined by the stakeholder. The most appropriate research design is then incorporated to answer the stated questions. Logistically speaking, it is usually not feasible or relevant to utilize experimental research within a program evaluation; however, observational, survey, time-series approaches, or *regression point-displacement* designs (RPD; see Linden, Trochim, & Adams, 2006; Trochim & Campbell, 1996), can serve as strong design alternatives. It should be noted that most leaders in the field of evaluation agree that mixed methods is the best method to be used by evaluators. Creswell and Plano Clark's (2011) mixed method *multiphase design* is an ideal variant to be combined with program evaluation models. The reader is referred to Stufflebeam and Shinkfield (2007) for an in-depth review of evaluation models and applications.

PHILOSOPHICAL TENETS ♦

The goal of this guide is to provide practical applications and visual representations of the most common research designs in the fields of education and the social and behavioral sciences. We hope that the presentation of each design and the relevant applied example will encourage researchers to apply many of these theoretically sound designs, which, in our opinion, are underutilized (particularly mixed methods). As noted, it is an applied text, focused on presenting visual aids and real-world examples to illustrate the key points rather than covering foundational and theoretical issues. However, the importance and relevance of the theory and philosophy related to the various research methods should be noted. That is, there are many theoretical tenets and philosophical principles undergirding the use of a particular method and associated design. More specifically, quantitative researchers focus on testing an a priori theory with an emphasis on deductive reasoning, and they are more in line with postpositivism. Alternatively, qualitatively oriented researchers often utilize inductive reasoning (or abductive), which is reflective of constructivism. Mixed methods can be viewed more as pragmatic in that this form most efficiently combines both the philosophical approaches of inductive and deductive reasoning. Some researchers would argue that all research should include mixed methods in that the form addresses the complexity of current research problems and counteracts the limitations inherent in utilizing only one type of method. The reader is referred to Creswell (2009) for an in-depth overview of philosophical approaches to quantitative, qualitative, and mixed methods.

◆ DATA ANALYTICS

We want to emphasize again that referring to the research designs presented in this reference guide as "common" can be misleading and does not mean that the designs are less powerful or that the results yielded will have less meaning. Practical and statistical significance can be ensured so long as validity is secured throughout the process (i.e., instrumentation, data collection, analysis, and reporting) and an adequate number of data points and participants are included (i.e., statistical power). Issues related to statistical power and determining the number of participants to include in any given study can be reviewed in Kraemer and Thiemann (1987) and a freeware program called G*Power (Erdfelder, Faul, & Buchner, 1996). It is also important to note that the statistical or data analytic techniques are driven by (a) the research questions or hypotheses and (b) the research design of choice. After the presentation of each design, we recommend the most appropriate statistical procedure (parametric) to be utilized, and we offer recommendations of data analytic software for qualitative methods. Statistical procedures will vary with the application of each design and there may be instances when nonparametric procedures should be applied. We refer the reader to Salkind and Green (2010) and Muijs (2010) for sound texts that detail statistical procedures and techniques using statistical software packages, as well as Pace (2011) for statistical applications utilizing Microsoft Excel. We also refer the reader to Bazeley (2007) for techniques related to qualitative data analyses.

◆ FINAL REMARKS

There are many different types of approaches to research (some considered to be more obscure) that are not research or method specific, and they are not discussed in this book. These include collaborative approaches such as (a) action research or participatory action research and appreciative inquiry; (b) systematic review approaches such as quantitative meta-analysis, qualitative metasynthesis, and metastudy; and (c) arts-based approaches such as auto-ethnography, portraiture, and life history (e.g., Butler-Kisber, 2010). These approaches can be applied with quantitative, qualitative, or mixed methods. Regardless of the type of approach, method, or research, one should still adhere to the appropriate tenets of scientific inquiry when examining phenomena in education and the social and behavioral sciences. Although not all types of research are aimed specifically at establishing cause and effect links, at some level all researchers should consider Cook and Campbell's (1979) three conditions for establishing cause and effect: (a) covariation (the change in the cause must be related to the effect), (b) temporal precedence (the cause must precede the effect), and (c) no plausible alternative explanations (the cause must be the only explanation for the effect). Implementing sound research designs is one of the primary steps in controlling for the issues related to plausible alternative explanations and satisfying the required conditions. It should be noted that Cook and Campbell mentioned that their research designs should not be used as templates, rather as guides to initiate inquiry.

However, based on many years of research and substantiation of the designs presented herein, these are some of the strongest designs applied within education and the social and behavioral sciences. Therefore, researchers can utilize and apply these designs as presented, with no modifications. Furthermore, each design can be modified to suit the primary stated research question. For example, a series of posttest observations can be added to the basic pretest and posttest control group design as a means to include a time-series component (see designs found in the repeated-measures approach for examples), or a researcher can integrate and combine various methodological and design components in the application of qualitative methods (as discussed with the generic design). Nonetheless, decisions such as these should be based on theoretical tenets and logistical considerations, and we stress that researchers utilize the most appropriate and parsimonious research design to answer the stated research questions. We also emphasize that researchers employ clarity and consistency when discussing the research design in written research reports and manuscripts submitted for publication. Consistency in terminology and clear descriptions of the design provide the reader with the necessary insight and understanding of the examination at hand.

Appendix A

Less Common Designs for Experimental and Quasi-Experimental Research

The designs presented here in Appendix A (Examples 1–9) are less commonly used but can be useful and appropriate under the correct circumstances. Some of these designs can be considered *pattern matching designs* (i.e., combining various design features into one design to improve the overall internal validity). These designs are structured for a variety of research scenarios when it is not logistically possible to utilize random assignment. The addition of various types of comparison groups and the addition of multiple pretest or posttest measures strengthens these research designs (in terms of internal validity) for various applications of quasi-experimental research. These "quasi-experimental" research designs are particularly ideal for researchers conducting examinations in the educational sector, considering that random assignment is rarely feasible. Examples A5, A10, and A11 are designs for experimental research rarely applied in the social sciences, but they are considered strong designs.

Example A1 Proxy Pretest-Posttest Design

Group	Assignment	Proxy Pretest	Treatment	Posttest
1	NR	O_{A1}	X	O_{B1}
2	NR	O_{A1}	—	O_{B1}

Time ▶

Note: This is an example of a between-subjects approach with a proxy pretest and posttest control group design. The proxy pretest allows the researcher to compare the "treatment effects" of O_{B1} to a proxy variable (O_{A1}). This design is useful when a program or intervention has already started and the researcher was not able to collect the same pretest measure that is being collected for the posttest. Therefore, data (archived) from a proxy variable can be collected that is considered conceptually similar to the posttest and can closely estimate pretest performance. For example, if a reading intervention is being implemented and a reading achievement test is being collected for the posttest, then a possible proxy variable would be the students' GPA prior to the intervention. Although the proxy pretest provides a measure of control, selection bias remains a major threat to the internal validity of this design.

Example A2 Double Pretest and Posttest Control Group Design

Group	Assignment	Pretest	Pretest	Treatment	Posttest
1	NR	O_1	O_2	X	O_3
2	NR	O_1	O_2	—	O_3

Time ▶

Note: This is an example of a between-subjects approach with a double pretest and posttest control group design. The double pretest allows the researcher to compare the "treatment effects" between O_1 to O_2, and then from O_2 to O_3. A major threat to internal validity with this design is testing, but it controls for selection bias and maturation.

Example A3 Pretest and Posttest Historical Control Group With a Pretest and Posttest Design

Group	Assignment	Pretest	Posttest	Pretest	Treatment	Posttest
1	NR	O_1	O_2	—	—	—
2	NR	—	—	O_1	X	O_2

Time ▶

Note: This is an example of a between-subjects approach with a pretest and posttest historical control group and pretest and posttest design. The historical control group allows the researcher to compare the "treatment effects" between O_1 to O_2 from the historical control to O_1 to O_2 of the treatment group. History and selection bias are the two most prevalent threats to the internal validity of this design.

Example A4 Posttest Only With a Historical Control Group Design

Group	Assignment	Test	Treatment	Posttest
1	NR	O_1	—	—
2	NR	—	X	O_1

Time ▶

Note: This design would be designated as quasi-experimental research utilizing a between-subjects approach with a posttest only and a historical control group design. History and selection bias would be the biggest threats to internal validity.

Example A5 Pretest and Posttest Control Group Plus Historical Control Group Design

Group	Assignment	Test	Pretest	Treatment	Posttest
1	R	—	O_1	X	O_2
2	R	—	O_1	—	O_2
3	NR	O_1	—	—	—

Time ▶

Note: This is an example of a between-subjects approach pretest and posttest control group design with the addition of a historical control group. The pretest and posttest aspect can be applied with or without random assignment. The historical control is typically a cohort control and helps to control for testing effects, which is a major threat to internal validity in designs that include pretest measures.

Example A6 Regression Point-Displacement (RPD) Design

Unit	Assignment	Pretest	Treatment	Posttest
1	NR	O_1	X	O_2
2*	NR	O_1	—	O_2

Time ▶

Note: This is an example of a between-subjects approach with a pretest and posttest control group RPD design. This design is best utilized for program evaluations or community-based research. It is difficult to infer causation in community-based examinations based on the evaluation of a single unit (or community) using the basic one-group pretest and posttest design. Therefore, for the comparison unit (2*), data can be collected from a heterogeneous set of units (or communities) and then collapsed and compared to the single unit that received the treatment. If logistically feasible, a time-series component can be added with a series of multiple pretests and posttests. A form of regression analysis is used to analyze the results. We refer the reader to Trochim and Campbell (1996) and Linden, Trochim, and Adams (2006) for further explanations on the RPD design and the most common threats to the internal validity of this design.

Example A7 One-Group Double Pretest and Posttest Design

Group	Assignment	Pretest	Pretest	Treatment	Posttest
1	NR	O_1	O_2	X	O_3

Time ▶

Note: This is an example of a one-group within-subjects approach with a double pretest and posttest design. The double pretest allows the researcher to compare the "treatment effects" between O_1 to O_2, and then from O_2 to O_3. A major threat to internal validity with this design is history, but it controls for testing and maturation. The one-group design is not considered as strong as the two-group variant of this design.

Example A8 One-Group Treatment-Removed Design

Group	Assignment	Pretest	Treatment	Midtest		Midtest	Treatment	Posttest
1	NR	O_1	X	O_2	Time Delay	O_3	—	O_4

Time ▶

Note: This is an example of a one-group pretest multiple posttest with the treatment-removed design. The goal of this design is to establish the change in the outcome based on the presence or absence of the treatment. Therefore, the researcher would assess the change from O_1 to O_2 and compare that to the change from O_3 to O_4, hypothesizing that in the absence of the treatment, the outcome would move in the opposite direction compared to that when it is present. It is assumed that the effects of the treatment should be expected to dissipate over time. Due to the lack of a comparison group, a variable (confounding) not controlled for can account for the change in the outcome; therefore, a large sample is required in order to minimize the negative impact on the statistical conclusion validity.

Example A9 One-Group Repeated-Treatment Design

Group	Assignment	Pretest	Treatment	Posttest	Treatment	Midtest	Treatment	Posttest
1	NR	O_1	X	O_2	—	O_3	X	O_4

Time ▶

Note: This is an example of a one-group pretest and posttest design repeated over time. The aim of this design is to verify that the change from O_1 to O_2 is similar in change from O_3 to O_4, hypothesizing that in the absence of the treatment, the outcome will move in the opposite direction between O_2 and O_3. The effects of the treatment implemented should be expected to dissipate over time, and the researcher should include a considerable delay between the initial treatment and the second application. Due to the lack of a comparison group, a variable not controlled for can account for the change in the outcome; therefore, a large sample is required in order to minimize the negative impact on the statistical conclusion validity. Testing, maturation, and history are major threats to the internal validity of this design.

Example A10 3-Factor Crossover Design

Group	Assignment	Pretest	Treatment	Midtest	Treatment	Midtest	Treatment	Posttest
1	R	O_1	X_A	O_2	X_B	O_3	X_C	O_4
2	R	O_1	X_B	O_2	X_A	O_3	X_C	O_4
3	R	O_1	X_C	O_2	X_A	O_3	X_B	O_4

Time ▶

Note: This is an example of a repeated-measures approach 3-factor crossover design. Each group serves in one condition and the conditions are counterbalanced to control for sequencing effects. This design can be modified in multiple ways, such as adding additional factors, introducing the same factor more than once in each condition, and including more observations. The variation of treatment orders can go up to 12 while including one participant per condition ($N = 12$). Based on this variation, the participant serves as his or her own control, which is an intended feature built into designs for repeated-measures approaches.

Example A11 3 × 3 Graeco-Latin Square Design

Blocking Factor (levels 1–3)	*Blocking Factor (levels 1–3)*		
	1	2	3
1	A_α	B_γ	C_β
2	B_β	C_α	A_γ
3	C_γ	A_β	B_α

Note: This is an example of a 3 × 3 Graeco-Latin square design. Similar to the Latin square design, this design is a one-factor model, but instead of two blocking factors, it includes a third extraneous factor and is denoted as α, γ, and β. As with the Latin square design, this design is best suited for research in agriculture and engineering; few scenarios warrant the use of such a design within the social sciences. In addition, with the use of human subjects, sequencing effects is a major threat to the internal validity of this design application. The analysis of means (ANOM) is the appropriate analysis for this design.

Appendix B

Types of Case Study Designs

Case Study Designs: Creswell (2012)

Creswell (2012) placed the case study within the ethnographic approach; however, the case study can be applied within the framework of any of the approaches detailed under qualitative methods.

Type	Definition
Intrinsic	The examination of a unique case
Instrumental	The examination of a case to provide insight into an issue or specific theme
Multiple Instrumental (also known as Collective Case Study)	The examination approach, which is the same as Instrumental but with multiple cases

Case Study Designs: Yin (2009)

According to Yin (2009), *holistic* refers to identifying and collecting data from a single unit of analysis, whereas *embedded* refers to collecting data from multiple units of analysis. Yin also indicated that his case study designs can be categorized and conducted as exploratory, descriptive, or explanatory (causal) investigations.

Type	Definition
Single Case–Holistic	
Critical case	Examine a well-formulated theory.
Unique case	Examine an extreme case.
Representative case	Examine a typical or average case.
Revelatory case	Examine a phenomenon that was previously inaccessible.
Longitudinal case	Examine the same cover over a period of time.
Single Case–Embedded	
Critical case	Examine a well-formulated theory.
Unique case	Examine an extreme case.
Representative case	Examine a typical or average case.
Revelatory case	Examine a phenomenon that was previously inaccessible.
Longitudinal case	Examine the same cover over a period of time.
Multiple Case–Holistic	
Literal replication	Select and examine each case so that all cases are presumed to predict similar results.
Theoretical replication	Select and examine each case so that all cases are presumed to predict contrasting results, but for anticipatable reasons.
Multiple Case–Embedded	
Literal replication	Select and examine each case so that all cases are presumed to predict similar results.
Theoretical replication	Select and examine each case so that all cases are presumed to predict contrasting results, but for anticipatable reasons.

Appendix C

Five Types of Mixed Methods Designs

Families of Mixed Methods Designs (Tashakkori & Teddlie, 2010a)	
Design	*Procedures*
Parallel mixed	• Mixing occurs in a parallel manner. • Data are collected simultaneously (or with some time lapse). • QUAL and QUAN phases answer related aspects of the same research questions.
Sequential mixed	• Mixing occurs across chronological phases (QUAL, QUAN). • Questions or procedures from one method emerge from, or depend on, the one prior. • Research questions are related to one another and may evolve.
Conversion mixed	• Parallel design is used. • Mixing occurs when one type of data is transformed and analyzed both qualitatively and quantitatively. • This is used to answer related aspects of the same research questions.
Multilevel mixed	• Parallel or sequential design is used. • Mixing occurs across multiple levels of analysis. • QUAN and QUAL data from these different levels are analyzed and integrated to answer aspects of the same (or related) research questions.
Fully integrated mixed	• Mixing occurs in an interactive manner at all stages of the study. • At each stage, one approach affects the formulation of the other. • Multiple types of implementation processes occur.

Note: Tashakkori & Teddlie (2010a) also present a quasi-mixed design (monostrand conversion design), where the "mixed" aspect refers to the *quantitizing* or *qualitizing* of data. In other words, the researcher would convert ("mix") one form of data (QUAL) to another form (QUAN) and only use the converted form of the data (QUAN or QUAL) to answer the research questions.

References

Abrams, L. S., Shannon, S. K. S., & Sangalang, C. (2008). Transition services for incarcerated youth: A mixed methods evaluation study. *Children and Youth Services Review, 30,* 522–535.

Acee, T. W., & Weinstein, C. E. (2010). Effects of value-reappraisal intervention on statistics students' motivation and performance. *Journal of Experimental Education, 78*(4), 487–512.

Basadur, M., Graen, G. B., & Scandura, T. A. (1986). Training effects on attitudes toward divergent thinking among manufacturing engineers. *Journal of Applied Psychology, 71*(4), 612–617.

Baylor, A. L., & Kim, S. (2009). Designing nonverbal communication for pedagogical agents: When less is more. *Computers in Human Behavior, 25,* 450–457.

Bazeley, P. (2007). *Qualitative data analysis with NVivo.* Thousand Oaks, CA: Sage.

Beeke, S., Wilkinson, R., & Maxin, J. (2007). Individual variation in agrammatism: A single case study of the influence of interaction. *Journal of Language and Communication Disorders, 42*(6), 629–647.

Berman, H., Mulcachy, G. A., Forchuk, C., Edmunds, K. A., Haldenby, A., & Lopez, R. (2009). Uprooted and displaced: A critical narrative study of homeless, aboriginal, and newcomer girls in Canada. *Issues in Mental Health Nursing, 30*(7), 418–430.

Bernard, R. S., Cohen, L. L., & Moffett, K. (2008). A token economy for exercise adherence in pediatric cystic fibrosis: A single-subject analysis. *Journal of Pediatric Psychology, 34*(4), 354–365.

Birks, M., Chapman, Y., & Francis, K. (2008). Memoing in qualitative research: Probing data and processes. *Journal of Research in Nursing, 13*(1), 68–75.

Box, G. E. P., Hunter, J. S., & Hunter, W. G. (2005). *Statistics for experimenters: Design, innovation and discovery.* Hoboken, NJ: Wiley.

Bryant, D. P., Bryant, B. R., Gersten, R., Scammacca, N., & Chavez, M. M. (2008). Mathematic intervention for first- and second-grade students with mathematics difficulties: The effects of tier 2 intervention delivered at booster lessons. *Remedial and Special Education, 29*(1), 20–31.

Burgess, G., Grogan, S., & Burwitz, L. (2006). Effects of a 6-week aerobic dance intervention on body image and physical self-perceptions in adolescent girls. *Body Image, 3,* 57–66.

Butler-Kisber, L. (2010). *Qualitative inquiry: Thematic, narrative and art-informed perspectives.* Thousand Oaks, CA: Sage.

Campbell, D. T. (1957). Factors relevant to the validity of experiments in social settings. *Psychological Bulletin, 54,* 297–312.

Campbell, D. T., & Stanley, J. C. (1963). *Experimental and quasi-experimental designs for research.* Skokie, IL: Rand McNally.

Cernin, P. A., & Lichtenberg, P. A. (2009). Behavioral treatment for depressed mood: A pleasant events intervention for seniors residing in assisted living. *Clinical Gerontologist, 32,* 324–331.

Chao, P., Bryan, T., Burstein, K., & Ergul, C. (2006). Family-centered intervention for young children at-risk for language and behavior problems. *Early Childhood Education Journal, 34*(2), 147–153.

Chapin, M. H., & Holbert, D. (2009). Differences in affect, life satisfaction, and depression between successfully and unsuccessfully rehabilitated persons with spinal cord injuries. *Rehabilitation Counseling Bulletin, 53*(1), 6–15.

Charmaz, K. (2006). *Constructing grounded theory: A practical guide through qualitative analysis.* London, England: Sage.

Chenail, R. (2010). Getting specific about qualitative research generalizability. *Journal of Ethnographic & Qualitative Research, 5,* 1–11.

Clandinin, D. J., & Connelly, F. M. (2000). *Narrative inquiry: Experience and story in qualitative research.* San Francisco, CA: Wiley.

Collins, K. M. T., & O'Cathain, A. (2009). Ten points about mixed methods research to be considered by the novice researcher. *International Journal of Multiple Research Approaches, 3*(1), 2–7.

Comaskey, E. M., Savage, R. S., & Abrami, P. (2009). A randomized efficacy study of web-based synthetic and analytic programmes among disadvantaged urban kindergarten children. *Journal of Research in Reading, 32*(1), 92–108.

Cook, T. D., & Campbell, D. T. (1979). *Quasi-Experimentation: Design and analysis issues for field settings.* Chicago, IL: Rand McNally.

Cook, T. D., & Steiner, P. M. (2010). Case matching and the reduction of selection bias in quasi-experiments: The relative importance of pretest measures of outcome, of unreliable measurement, and of mode of data analysis. *Psychological Methods, 15*(1), 56–68.

Corbin, J., & Strauss, A. (2007). *Basics of qualitative research: Techniques and procedures for developing grounded theory* (3rd ed.). Thousand Oaks, CA: Sage.

Creswell, J. W. (2007). *Qualitative inquiry and research design: Choosing among five approaches* (2nd ed.). Thousand Oaks, CA: Sage.

Creswell, J. W. (2009). *Research design: Qualitative, quantitative, and mixed methods approaches* (3rd ed.). Thousand Oaks, CA: Sage.

Creswell, J. W. (2012). *Educational research: Planning, conducting, and evaluating quantitative and qualitative research* (4th ed.). Upper Saddle River, NJ: Pearson.

Creswell, J. W., & Plano Clark, V. L. (2011). *Designing and conducting mixed methods research* (2nd ed.). Thousand Oaks, CA: Sage.

Cribbie, R. A., Arpin-Cribbie, C. A., & Gruman, J. A. (2010). Tests of equivalence for one-way independent groups designs. *The Journal of Experimental Education, 78,* 1–13.

Dennis, J. K. (2003). Problem-based learning in online vs. face-to-face environments. *Education for Health, 16*(2), 198–209.

DeVellis, R. F. (2003). *Scale development: Theory and applications* (2nd ed.). Thousand Oaks, CA: Sage.

Dixon, M. R., Jackson, J. W., Small, S. L., Horner-King, M. J., Lik, N. M. K, Garcia, Y., & Rosales, R. (2009). Creating single-subject design graphs in Microsoft Excel™ 2007. *Journal of Applied Behavior Analysis, 42*(2), 277–293.

Elliott, M. S., & Williams, D. I. (2002). A qualitative evaluation of an employee counselling service from the perspective of client, counselor, and organization. *Counselling Psychology Quarterly, 15*(2), 201–208.

Erdfelder, E., Faul, F., & Buchner, A. (1996). GPOWER: A general power analysis program. *Behavior Research Methods, Instruments, & Computers, 28,* 1–11.

Erdogan, Y., Aydin, E., & Kabaca, T. (2008). Exploring the psychological predictors of programming achievement. *Journal of Instructional Psychology, 35*(3), 264–270.

Fetterman, D. M. (2009). *Ethnography: Step-by-step* (3rd ed.). Thousand Oaks, CA: Sage.

Fink, A. G. (2009). *How to conduct surveys: A step-by-step guide* (4th ed.). Thousand Oaks, CA: Sage.

Forchuk, C., Norman, R., Malla, A., Martin, M., McLean, T., & Cheng, S., . . . Gibney, C. (2002). Schizophrenia and the motivation for smoking. *Perspectives in Psychiatric Care, 38*(2), 41–49.

Fowler, F. J. (2009). *Survey research methods* (4th ed.). Thousand Oaks, CA: Sage.

Gall, M. D., Gall, J. P., & Borg, W. R. (2007). *Educational research: An introduction.* Boston, MA: Pearson.

Ganz, J. B., & Flores, M. M. (2009). The effectiveness of direct instruction for teaching language to children with autism spectrum disorders: Identifying material. *Journal of Autism and Developmental Disorders, 39,* 75–83.

Geertz, C. (1998). The world in pieces: Cultural politics at the end of the century. *FOCAAL: European Journal of Anthropology, 32,* 91–117.

Gier, V. S., Kreiner, D. S., & Natz-Gonzalez, A. (2009). Harmful effects of preexisting inappropriate highlighting on reading comprehension and metacognitive accuracy. *The Journal of General Psychology, 136*(3), 287–300.

Giorgi, A. (2009). *The descriptive phenomenological method in psychology: A modified Huesserlian approach.* Pittsburgh, PA: Duquesne University Press.

Giuffre, M. (1997). Designing research: Ex post facto designs. *Journal of PeriAnesthesia Nursing, 12*(3), 191–195.

Glaser, B. G., & Strauss, A. L. (1967). *The discovery of grounded theory: Strategies for qualitative research.* Hawthorne, NY: Aldine Transaction.

Glass, V. G., Wilson, V. L., & Gottman, J. M. (2008). *Design and analysis of time-series experiments.* Charlotte, NC: Information Age Publishing.

Golafshani, N. (2003). Understanding reliability and validity in qualitative research. *The Qualitative Report, 8*(4), 597–607.

Green, M., & Cifuentes, L. (2008). An exploration of online environments supporting follow-up to face-to-face professional development. *Journal of Technology and Teacher Education, 16*(3), 283–306.

Guadagno, R. E., & Sagarin, B. J. (2010). Sex differences in jealousy: An evolutionary perspective on online infidelity. *Journal of Applied Social Psychology, 40*(10), 2636–2655.

Guba, E. G., & Lincoln, Y. S. (2005). Paradigmatic controversies, contradictions, and emerging influences. In N. K. Denzin & Y. S. Lincoln (Eds.), *The Sage handbook of qualitative research* (3rd ed., pp. 191–215). Thousand Oaks, CA: Sage.

Hall-Kenyon, K. M., Bingham, G. E., & Korth, B. B. (2009). How do linguistically diverse students fare in full- and half-day kindergarten? Examining academic achievement, instructional quality, and attendance. *Early Education and Development, 20,* 25–52.

Han, G. S., & Davies, C. (2006). Ethnicity, health and medical care: Towards a critical realist analysis of general practice in the Korean community in Sydney. *Ethnicity and Health, 11*(4), 409–430.

Hannan, M., Happ, M. B., & Charron-Prochownik, D. (2009). Mothers' perspectives about reproductive health discussion with adolescent daughters with diabetes. *The Diabetes Educator, 35*(2), 265–273.

Haydon, T., Mancil, G. R., & Van Loan, C. (2009). Using opportunities to respond in a general education classroom: A case study. *Education and Treatment of Children, 32*(2), 267–278.

Hedayat, A. S., Stufken, J., & Yang, M. (2006). Optimal and efficient crossover designs when subject effects are random. *Journal of the American Statistical Association, 101,* 1031–1038.

Hinkelman, K., & Kempthorne, K. (2005). *Design and analysis of experiments, Volume 2: Advanced experimental designs.* Hoboken, NJ: Wiley.

Hinnant, J. B., O'Brien, M., & Ghazarian, S. R. (2009). The longitudinal relations of teacher expectations to achievement in early school years. *Journal of Educational Psychology, 101*(3), 662–670.

Hirakata, P. (2009). Narratives of dissociation: Insights into the treatment of dissociation in individuals who were sexually abused as children. *Journal of Trauma & Dissociation, 10*(1), 297–314.

Imbens, G. W., & Lemieux, T. (2008). Regression discontinuity designs: A guide to practice. *Journal of Econometrics, 142,* 615–635.

Jaccard, J., & Jacoby, J. (2010). *Theory construction and model-building skills: A practical guide for social scientists.* New York, NY: Guilford Press.

Jones, M. A., Stratten, G., Reilly, T., & Unnithan, V. B. (2004). A school-based survey of recurrent non-specific low-back pain prevalence and consequences in children. *Health Education Research, 19*(3), 284–289.

Jones, S. R., & Hill, K. E. (2003). Understanding patterns of commitment: Student motivation for community service involvement. *Journal of Higher Education, 74*(5), 516–539.

Kaldjian, L. C., Jones, E. W., Rosenthal, G. E., Tripp-Reimer, T., & Hillis, S. L. (2006). An empirically derived taxonomy of factors affecting physicians' willingness to disclose medical errors. *Journal of General Internal Medicine, 21,* 942–948.

Kartalova-O'Doherty, Y., & Doherty, D. T. (2008). Coping strategies and styles of family carers of persons with enduring mental illness: A mixed methods analysis. *Scandinavian Journal of Caring Sciences, 22*(1), 19–28.

Kazdin, A. E. (2002). *Research designs in clinical psychology* (4th ed.). Needham Heights, MA: Allyn & Bacon.

Kazdin, A. E. (2010). *Single-case research designs: Methods for clinical and applied settings.* New York, NY: Oxford University Press.

Kazdin, A. E., Esveldt-Dawson, K., French, N. H., & Unis, A. S. (1987). Problem-solving skills training and relationship therapy in the treatment of antisocial child behavior. *Journal of Counseling and Clinical Psychology, 55*(1), 76–85.

Keith, T. Z. (2006). *Multiple regression and beyond.* Boston, MA: Pearson.

Kennedy, C. H. (2005). *Single-case designs for educational research.* Boston, MA: Pearson.

Kline, R. B. (2010). *Principles and practice of structural equation modeling* (3rd ed.). New York, NY. Guilford Press.

Kraemer, H. C., & Thiemann, S. (1987). *How many subjects?: Statistical power analysis in research.* Thousand Oaks, CA: Sage.

Kramarski, B., & Mevarech, Z. R. (2003). Enhancing mathematical reasoning in the classroom: The effects of cooperative learning and metacognitive training. *American Educational Research Journal, 40*(1), 281–310.

Lachin, J. M., Matts, J. P., & Wei, L. J. (1988). Randomization in clinical trials: Conclusions and recommendations. *Controlled Clinical Trials, 9,* 365–374.

Lapadat, J. C. (2004). Autobiographical memories of early language and literacy development. *Narrative Inquiry, 14*(1), 113–140.

Lavrakas, P. J. (Ed.). (2009). *Encyclopedia of survey research methods.* Thousand Oaks, CA: Sage.

Leake, M., & Lesik, S. A. (2007). Do remedial English programs impact first-year success in college? An illustration of the regression-discontinuity design. *International Journal of Research & Method in Education, 30*(1), 89–99.

Lee, K. S., Osborne, R. E., Hayes, K. A., & Simoes, R. A. (2008). The effects of pacing on the academic testing performance of college students with ADHD: A mixed methods study. *Journal of Educational Computing Research, 39*(2), 123–141.

Lee, Y., Park, S., Kim, M., Son, C., & Lee, M. (2005). The effects of visual illustrations on learners' achievement and interest in PDA- (personal digital assistant) based learning. *Journal of Educational Computing Research, 33*(2), 173–187.

Lesik, S. A. (2006). Applying the regression-discontinuity design to infer causality with non-random assignment. *The Review of Higher Education, 30*(1), 1–19.

Lesik, S. A. (2008). Studying the effectiveness of programs and initiatives in higher education using the regression-discontinuity design. *Handbook of Theory and Research, 23,* 277–297.

Levy, P. S., & Lemeshow, S. (2009). *Sampling of populations: Methods and applications* (4th ed.). New York, NY: Wiley.

Lieblich, A., Tuval-Mashiach, R., & Zilber, T. (1998). *Narrative research: Reading, analysis, and interpretation.* Thousand Oaks, CA: Sage.

Linden, A., Trochim, W. M. K., & Adams, J. L. (2006). Evaluating program effectiveness using the regression point displacement design. *Evaluation & the Health Professions, 29*(4), 407–423.

Lopez, E. N., Drobes, D. J., Thompson, K. J., & Brandon, T. H. (2008). Effects of body image challenge on smoking motivation among college females. *Health Psychology, 27*(3), 243–251.

Luytena, H., Tymms, P., & Jones, P. (2009). Assessing school effects without controlling for prior achievement? *School Effectiveness and School Improvement, 20*(2), 145–165.

Lyon, A. R., Gershenson, R. A., Farahmand, F. K., Thaxter, P. J., Behling, S., & Budd, K. S. (2009). Effectiveness of teacher-child interaction training (TCIT) in a preschool setting. *Behavior Modification, 33*(6), 855–884.

Madison, D. S. (2005). *Critical ethnography: Methods, ethics, and performance.* Thousand Oaks, CA: Sage.

Maguire, P. (1987). *Doing participatory research: A feminist approach.* Amherst, MA: Center for International Education.

Makagon, D., & Neumann, M. (2009). *Recording culture.* Thousand Oaks, CA: Sage.

Malcolm, T. (2010). The curious case of case study: A viewpoint. *International Journal of Social Research Methodology: Theory and Practice, 13*(4), 329–339.

Mancil, G. R., Haydon, T., & Whitby, P. (2009). Differential effects of paper and computer-assisted Social Stories™ on inappropriate behavior in children with autism. *Focus on Autism and Other Developmental Disabilities, 24*(4), 205–215.

Manolov, R., Solanas, A., Bulté, I., & Onghena, P. (2010). Data-division-specific robustness and power of randomization tests for ABAB designs. *Journal of Experimental Education, 78,* 191–214.

May, H., & Supovitz, J. A. (2006). Capturing the cumulative effects of school reform: An 11-year study of the impacts of America's choice on student achievement. *Educational Evaluation and Policy Analysis, 28*(3), 231–257.

McAdams, D. P., Josselson, R., & Lieblich, A. (2006). *Identity and story: Creating self in narrative.* Washington, DC: American Psychological Association.

McCarthy, A. M., & Tucker, M. L. (2002). Encouraging community service through service learning. *Journal of Management Education, 26*(6), 629–647.

McNemar, Q. (2007). On the use of Latin squares in psychology. *Psychological Bulletin, 48*(5), 398–401.

Meijer, J., & Oostdam, R. (2007). Test anxiety and intelligence testing: A closer examination of the stage-fright hypothesis and the influence of stressful instruction. *Anxiety, Stress, and Coping, 20*(1), 77–91.

Moerer-Urdahl, T., & Creswell, J. W. (2004). Using transcendental phenomenology to explore the "ripple effect" in a leadership mentoring program. *International Journal of Qualitative Methods, 3*(2), 19–35.

Morgan, B. J. (2001). Evaluation of an educational intervention for military tobacco users. *Military Medicine, 166*(12), 1094–1098.

Morse, J. M. (1991). Approaches to qualitative-quantitative methodological triangulation. *Nursing Research, 40,* 120–123.

Morse, J. M., & Niehaus, L. (2009). *Mixed methods design: Principles and procedures.* Walnut Creek, CA: Left Coast Press.

Moustakas, C. (1994). *Phenomenological research methods.* Thousand Oaks, CA: Sage.

Muijs, D. (2010). *Doing quantitative research in education with SPSS* (2nd ed.). Thousand Oaks, CA: Sage.

Nagel, T., Robinson, G., Condon, J., & Trauer, T. (2009). Approach to treatment of mental illness and substance dependence in remote indigenous communities: Results of a mixed methods study. *Australian Journal of Rural Health, 17*(4), 174–182.

Nastasi, B. K., Hitchcock, J., Sarkar, S., Burkholder, G., Varjas, K., & Jayasena, A. (2007). Mixed methods in intervention research: Theory to adaptation. *Journal of Mixed Methods Research, 1*(2), 164–183.

O'Neill, R. E., McDonnell, J. J., Billingsley, F. F., & Jenson, W. R. (2010). *Single case research designs in educational and community settings.* Upper Saddle River, NJ: Pearson.

Pace, L. A. (2011). *Statistical analysis using Excel 2007.* Upper Saddle River, NJ: Prentice Hall.

Patton, M. Q. (2002). *Qualitative research and evaluation methods* (3rd ed.). Thousand Oaks, CA: Sage.

Plano Clark, V. L. (2005). Cross-disciplinary analysis of the use of mixed methods in physics education research, counseling psychology, and primary care. *Dissertation Abstracts International, 66,* 02A.

Polkinghorne, D. E. (1988). *Narrative knowing and the human sciences.* Albany: State University of New York Press.

Pollio, H. R., Henley, T., & Thompson, C. B. (1997). *The phenomenology of everyday life.* Cambridge, UK: Cambridge University Press.

Prinzie, P., & Onghena, P. (2005). Cohort sequential design. In B. S. Everrit & D. Howell (Eds.), *Encyclopedia of statistics in behavioral science* (pp. 319–322). West Sussex, UK: Wiley-Blackwell.

Probst, T. M. (2003). Exploring employee outcomes of organizational restructuring. *Group & Organization Management, 28*(3), 416–439.

Purser, G. (2009). The dignity of job-seeking men: Boundary work among immigrant day laborers. *Journal of Contemporary Ethnography, 38*(1), 117–139.

Ragin, C. C. (1997). Turning the tables: How case-oriented research challenges variable-oriented research. *Comparative Social Research, 16,* 27–42.

Reese, H. W. (1997). Counterbalancing and other uses of repeated-measures Latin-square designs: Analysis and interpretations. *Journal of Experimental Child Psychology, 64,* 137–158.

Richardson, J. B. (2009). Men do matter: Ethnographic insights on the socially supportive role of the African American uncle in the lives of inner-city African American male youth. *Journal of Family Issues, 30*(8), 1041–1069.

Riessman, C. K. (2007). *Narrative methods for the human sciences.* Thousand Oaks, CA: Sage.

Rihoux, B., & Lobe, B. (2009). The case for qualitative comparative analysis (QCA): Adding leverage for thick cross-case comparison. In D. Byrne & C. C. Ragin (Eds.), *The Sage handbook of case-based methods* (pp. 222–242). Thousand Oaks, CA: Sage.

Rimondini, M., Del Piccolo, L., Goss, C., Mazzi, M., Paccaloni, M., & Zimmerman, C. (2010). The evaluation of training in patient-centered interviewing skills for psychiatric residents. *Psychological Medicine, 40,* 467–476.

Rubin, D. B. (2006). *Matched sampling for causal effects.* Cambridge, UK: Cambridge University Press.

Rubin, D. B. (2007). The design versus the analysis of observational studies for causal effects: Parallels with the design of randomized trials. *Statistics in Medicine, 26*(1), 20–36.

Rubin, D. B. (2008). For objective causal inference, design trumps analysis. *The Annals of Applied Statistics, 2*(3), 808–840.

Ryan, T. P. (2007). *Modern experimental design.* Hoboken, NJ: Wiley.

Ryndak, D. L., Storch, J. F., & Hoppey, D. (2008). One family's perspective of their experiences with school and district personnel over time related to inclusive educational services for a family member with significant disabilities. *International Journal of Whole Schooling, 4*(2), 29–51.

Salkind, N. J., & Green, S. (2010). *SPSS quick start.* Upper Saddle River, NJ: Prentice Hall.

Sawilowsky, S., Kelley, D. L., Blair, R. C., & Markman, B. S. (1994). Meta-analysis and the Solomon four-group design. *Journal of Experimental Education, 62,* 361–376.

Schoenfeld, N. A., & Mathur, S. R. (2009). Effects of cognitive-behavioral intervention on the school performance of students with emotional or behavioral disorders and anxiety. *Behavioral Disorders, 34*(4), 184–195.

Seifert, T. A., Goodman, K., King, P. M., & Baxter Magolda, M. B. (2010). Using mixed methods to study first-year college impact on liberal arts learning outcomes. *Journal of Mixed Methods Research, 4*(3), 248–267.

Shadish, W. R. (2010). Campbell and Rubin: A primer and comparison of their approaches to causal inference in field settings. *Psychological Methods, 15,* 3–17.

Shadish, W. R., Clark, M. H., & Steiner, P. M. (2008). Can nonrandomized experiments yield accurate answers? A randomized experiment comparing random to nonrandom assignment. *Journal of the American Statistical Association, 103,* 1334–1344.

Shadish, W. R., & Cook, T. D. (2009). The renaissance of field experimentation in evaluating interventions. *The Annual Review of Psychology, 60,* 607–629.

Shadish, W. R., Cook, T. D., & Campbell, D. T. (2002). *Experimental and quasi-experimental designs for generalized causal inference.* Boston, MA: Houghton Mifflin.

Shin, K. R. (2002). Using hermeneutic phenomenology to elicit a sense of body at mid-life. *International Journal of Qualitative Methods, 1*(2), 39–50.

Sidani, Y. M. (2007). Perceptions of leader transformational ability: The role of leader speech and follower self-esteem. *Journal of Management Development, 26*(8), 710–722.

Singer, J. A. (1997). *Message in a bottle: Stories of men and addiction.* New York, NY: Free Press.

Singer, J. A., & Bonalume, L. (2010a). Toward the scientific study of autobiographical memory narratives in psychotherapy. *Pragmatic Case Studies in Psychotherapy, 6,* 215–222.

Singer, J. A., & Bonalume, L. (2010b). Autobiographical memory narratives in psychotherapy: A coding system applied to the case of Cynthia. *Pragmatic Case Studies in Psychotherapy, 6,* 134–188.

Smith, J. A., Flowers, P., & Larkin, M. (2009). *Interpretive phenomenological analysis: Theory, method, and research.* Thousand Oaks, CA: Sage.

Smith, M. E. (2007). Self-deception among men who are mandated to attend a batterer intervention program. *Perspectives in Psychiatric Care, 43*(4), 193–203.

Solomon, R. L. (1949). An extension of the control group design. *Psychological Bulletin, 46,* 137–150.

Spector, P. E. (1981). *Research designs.* Beverly Hills, CA: Sage.

Spradley, J. P. (1979). *The ethnographic interview.* New York, NY: Holt, Rinehart & Winston.

Spradley, J. P. (1980). *Participant observation.* New York, NY: Holt, Rinehart & Winston.

Steinfield, C., Ellison, N. B., & Lampe, C. (2008). Social capital, self-esteem, and use of online social network sites: A longitudinal analysis. *Journal of Applied Developmental Psychology, 29,* 434–445.

Stern, S. E., Mullennix, J. W., & Wilson, S. J. (2002). Effects of perceived disability on persuasiveness of computer-synthesized speech. *Journal of Applied Psychology, 87*(2), 411–417.

Stewart, A. L., King, A. C., & Haskell, W. L. (1993). Endurance exercise and health-related quality of life in 50-65 year-old adults. *The Gerontologist, 33*(6), 782–789.

Steyn, R. (2009). Re-designing the Solomon four-group: Can we improve on this exemplary model? *Design Principles and Practices: An International Journal, 3*(1), 1833–1874.

Stufflebeam, D. L., & Shinkfield, A. J. (2007). *Evaluation theory, models, & applications.* San Francisco, CA: Jossey-Bass.

Tashakkori, A., & Teddlie, C. B. (2002). *Mixed methodology: Combining qualitative and quantitative approaches.* Thousand Oaks, CA: Sage.

Tashakkori, A., & Teddlie, C. B. (2010a). *SAGE handbook of mixed methods in social & behavioral research* (2nd ed.). Thousand Oaks, CA: Sage.

Tashakkori, A., & Teddlie, C. B. (2010b). Putting the human back into "human research methodology": The researcher in mixed methods research. *Journal of Mixed Methods Research, 4*(4), 271–277.

Thomas, J. (1993). *Doing critical ethnography.* Newbury Park, CA: Sage.

Todman, J. B., & Dugard, P. (2001). *Single-case and small-n experimental designs: A practical guide to randomization tests.* Mahwah, NJ: Lawrence Erlbaum Associates.

Trochim, W. (2001). Regression-discontinuity design. In N. J. Smelser, J. D. Wright, & P. B. Baltes (Eds.), *International encyclopedia of the social and behavioral sciences* (Vol. 19, pp. 12940–12945). North-Holland, Amsterdam: Pergamon.

Trochim, W., & Campbell, D. T. (1996). *The regression point displacement design for evaluating community-based pilot programs and demonstration projects.* Unpublished manuscript. Retrieved from http://www.socialresearchmethods.net/research/RPD/RPD.pdf

Trochim, W., & Cappelleri, J. C. (1992). Cutoff assignment strategies for enhancing randomized clinical trials. *Controlled Clinical Trials, 13,* 190–212.

Van Maanen, J. (1988). *Tales of the field: On writing ethnography.* Chicago, IL: University of Chicago Press.

Van Manen, M. (1990). *Researching lived experience: Human science for an action sensitive pedagogy.* Albany: The State University of New York.

Varcoe, C., Browne, A. J., Wong, S., & Smye, V. L. (2009). Harms and benefits: Collecting ethnicity data in a clinical context. *Social Science & Medicine, 68,* 1659–1666.

Villalta-Gil, V., Roca, M., Gonzales, N., Domènec, E., Cuca, Escanilla, A., . . . Haro, J. M. (2009). Dog-assisted therapy in the treatment of chronic schizophrenia inpatients. *Antrozoös, 22*(2), 149–159.

Viswanathan, M. (2005). *Measurement error and research design.* Thousand Oaks, CA: Sage.

Vogt, W. P. (2005). *Dictionary of statistics and methodology: A non-technical guide for the social sciences* (3rd ed.). Thousand Oaks, CA: Sage.

von Eckartsberg, R. (1997). Introducing existential-phenomenological psychology. In R. Valle (Ed.), *Phenomenological inquiry in psychology: Existential and transpersonal dimensions* (pp. 3–20). New York, NY: Plenum.

Walker, C. O., & Greene, B. A. (2009). The relations between student motivational beliefs and cognitive engagement in high school. *Journal of Educational Research, 102*(6), 463–471.

Walton Braver, M. C., & Braver, S. L. (1988). Statistical treatment of the Solomon four-group design: A meta-analytic approach. *Psychological Bulletin, 104*(1), 150–154.

Wertz, F. J., Charmaz, K., McMullen, L. M., Josselson, R., Anderson, R., & Emalinda, M. (2011). *Five ways of doing qualitative analysis: Phenomenological psychology, grounded theory, discourse analysis, narrative research, and intuitive inquiry.* New York, NY: Guilford Press.

White, P. (2009). *Developing research questions: A guide for social scientists.* New York, NY: Palgrave Macmillan.

Whitman, D. S., Van Rooy, D. L., Viswesvaran, C., & Alonso, A. (2008). The susceptibility of a mixed model measure of emotional intelligence to faking: A Solomon four-group design. *Psychology Science, 50*(1), 44–63.

Williams, E. N., & Morrow, S. L. (2009). Achieving trustworthiness in qualitative research: A pan-paradigmatic perspective. *Psychotherapy Research, 19*(4 & 5), 576–582.

Wolcott, H. F. (1994). *Transforming qualitative data: Description, analysis, and interpretation.* Thousand Oaks, CA: Sage.

Wyatt, T. H., & Hauenstein, E. J. (2008). Pilot test Okay With Asthma™: An online asthma intervention for school-age children. *The Journal of School Nursing, 24*(3), 145–150.

Yin, R. K. (Ed.). (2004). *The case study anthology.* Thousand Oaks, CA: Sage.

Yin, R. K. (2009). *Case study research: Design and methods* (4th ed.). Thousand Oaks, CA: Sage.

Yin, R. K. (2012). *Applications of case study research* (3rd ed.). Thousand Oaks, CA: Sage.

Young, P., & Miller-Smith, K. (2006). Effects of state mandated policy (site-based councils) and of potential role incumbents on teacher screening decisions in high and low performing schools. *Education Policy and Analysis Archives, 14*(7), 1–21.

Zoffmann, V., & Kirkevold, M. (2007). Relationships and their potential for change developed in difficult type 1 diabetes. *Qualitative Health Research, 17*(5), 625–638.

Zolotor, A. J., Runyan, D. K., Dunne, M. P., Jain, D., Petrus, H. R., Ramirez, C., . . . Isaeva, O. (2009). ISPCAN Child Abuse Screening Tool Children's Version (ICAST-C): Instrument development and multi-national pilot testing. *Child Abuse & Neglect, 33*(11), 833–841.

Zydney, J. M. (2008). Cognitive tools for scaffolding students defining an ill-structured problem. *Journal of Educational Computing Research, 38*(4), 353–385.

Author Index

202

Subject Index

Note: Notes are indicated by n after the page number. Figures are indicated by (figure). Tables are indicated by (table).

⑧SAGE research methods online

The essential tool for researchers . . .

. . . from the world's leading research methods publisher

Discover SRMO Lists— methods readings suggested by other SRMO users

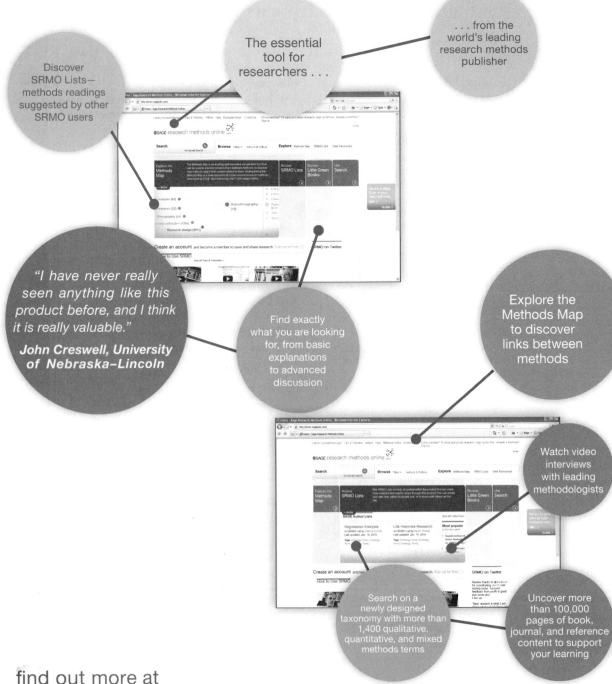

"I have never really seen anything like this product before, and I think it is really valuable."

John Creswell, University of Nebraska–Lincoln

Find exactly what you are looking for, from basic explanations to advanced discussion

Explore the Methods Map to discover links between methods

Watch video interviews with leading methodologists

Search on a newly designed taxonomy with more than 1,400 qualitative, quantitative, and mixed methods terms

Uncover more than 100,000 pages of book, journal, and reference content to support your learning

find out more at
www.srmo.sagepub.com